TRACING YOUR
MARGINALISED
ANCESTORS

This book is dedicated to the marginalised – past, present and future

TRACING YOUR MARGINALISED ANCESTORS
A GUIDE FOR FAMILY HISTORIANS

JANET FEW

Pen & Sword
FAMILY HISTORY

First published in Great Britain in 2024 by
PEN AND SWORD FAMILY HISTORY
An imprint of
Pen & Sword Books Ltd
Yorkshire – Philadelphia

Copyright © Janet Few, 2024

ISBN 978 1 39906 185 8

The right of Janet Few to be identified as Author of this work has been asserted by her in accordance with the Copyright, Designs and Patents Act 1988.

A CIP catalogue record for this book is available from the British Library

All rights reserved. No part of this book may be reproduced or transmitted in any form or by any means, electronic or mechanical including photocopying, recording or by any information storage and retrieval system, without permission from the Publisher in writing.

Typeset in 10/13 Palatino by SJmagic DESIGN SERVICES, India.
Printed and bound in the UK by CPI Group (UK) Ltd.

Pen & Sword Books Ltd incorporates the Imprints of Aviation, Atlas, Family History, Fiction, Maritime, Military, Discovery, Politics, History, Archaeology, Select, Wharncliffe Local History, Wharncliffe True Crime, Military Classics, Wharncliffe Transport, Leo Cooper, The Praetorian Press, Remember When, Seaforth Publishing and Frontline Publishing.

For a complete list of Pen & Sword titles please contact

PEN & SWORD BOOKS LTD
George House, Units 12 & 13, Beevor Street, Off Pontefract Road, Barnsley, South Yorkshire, S71 1HN, England
E-mail: enquiries@pen-and-sword.co.uk
Website: www.pen-and-sword.co.uk

or
PEN & SWORD BOOKS
1950 Lawrence Rd, Havertown, PA 19083, USA
E-mail: uspen-and-sword@casematepublishers.com
Website: www.penandswordbooks.com

CONTENTS

List of Illustrations vi
Acknowledgements ix
Introduction x

Chapter 1	Poverty 1	
	The Story of Harriet Bentlif 12	
Chapter 2	Criminality 14	
	The Story of Frederick Michael Railton 25	
Chapter 3	Immigration and Ethnicity 29	
	The Story of Catherine Eve 38	
Chapter 4	Prostitution 40	
	The Story of Charity Platt 47	
Chapter 5	Illegitimacy 50	
	The Story of Hannah Midgely 56	
Chapter 6	The Inebriate 58	
	The Story of Sarah Grosvenor 64	
Chapter 7	Sickness and Disability 68	
	The Story of Richard Gill and William Leathern 79	
Chapter 8	Mental Ill-Health 81	
	The Story of Fanny Amelia Ellington 90	
Chapter 9	The Romany and Traveller Community 93	
	The Story of Joshua Mobbs 99	
Chapter 10	Witchcraft 102	
	The Story of Susanna Edwards 110	
Chapter 11	Other Marginalised Groups 114	
	Religious Belief 114	
	Sexuality 117	
	Conscientious Objection and Desertion 119	
	The Story of William Wilcox 124	

References and Further Reading 126
Index 145

LIST OF ILLUSTRATIONS

Chapter 1: Poverty
Gressenhall Workhouse © Janet Few.

Applicants for Admission to a Casual Ward, Sir Luke Fildes. Tate Gallery Image released under Creative Commons CC-BY-NC-ND (3.0 Unported).

A Glasgow Slum, Thomas Annan 1861 British Library. Image in the public domain, accessed via Wikimedia Commons.

Chapter 2: Criminality
William Prynne in the Pillory, John Cassell 1865. Image in the public domain, accessed via Wikimedia Commons.

Ducking a Scold, an illustration from an eighteenth-century chap-book reproduced in *Chap-books of the eighteenth century*, John Ashton 1834. Image in the public domain, accessed via Wikimedia Commons.

The Prospect of Bridewell, from John Strype's *An Accurate Edition of Stow's Survey of London* 1720. Image in the public domain, accessed via Wikimedia Commons.

Cell with Prisoner at Crank-Labour in the Surrey House of Correction 1851, from *London Labour and the London Poor*, Henry Mayhew 1851. Image in the public domain, accessed via Wikimedia Commons.

Chapter 3: Immigration and Ethnicity
Emigrants Leave Ireland, by Henry Doyle (1827–1892), from Mary Frances Cusack's *Illustrated History of Ireland*, 1868. Image in the public domain.

The Alien Invasion, Immigrant Jews in the Transit Shed at Tilbury *c*.1891. Image in the public domain, accessed via Wikimedia Commons.

People with baskets and sacks pick cotton on a plantation. Coloured lithograph after J.R. Barfoot. The Wellcome Collection **https://wellcomecollection.org/works/mf7r354u** Used under Creative Commons CC-BY-4.0 licence. Also on the cover.

Chapter 4: Prostitution

Ladies National Association for the Repeal of the Contagious Diseases Acts, image in the public domain, accessed via Wikimedia Commons.

A Harlot's Progress, Hogarth. Image used under Creative Commons in the public domain. Also on the cover.

A Swell's Night Guide, c.1847. The British Library C.194.a.1217. Image in the public domain.

Chapter 5: Illegitimacy

The Birth certificate of Albany Braund, from the private collection of Janet Few.

The Foundling Hospital, Holborn, London: A Bird's-Eye View of The Courtyard Numbered for A Key, Coloured engraving after L.P. Boitard, 1753. The Wellcome Institute, library reference ICV13747, photo number V0013461 **https//catalogue.wellcomelibrary.org/record=b1194811**. Used under Creative Commons.

Chapter 6: The Inebriate

Gin Lane, William Hogarth. Image in the public domain, accessed via Wikimedia Commons.

Noah's Inebriation, Giovanni Andrea de Ferrari 1630s. Image in the public domain, accessed via Wikimedia Commons, used under Creative Commons CC0 1.0.

Wine is a Mocker, Jane Steen c.1663. Image in the public domain, accessed via Wikimedia Commons. Also on the cover.

Chapter 7: Sickness and Disability

Zodiac Man 1702. Image in the public domain, accessed via Wikimedia Commons.

Lungwort © Janet Few.

Dr Williams' Little Pink Pills, 1850–1920 Wellcome Images L0058211, Science Museum, London used under Creative Commons CC-BY-4.0.

Barber Surgeon's Tools © Janet Few.

Chapter 8: Mental Ill-Health

The Lunatic Asylum, unknown engraver, image in the public domain, accessed via Wikimedia Commons.

Casa de Locos, Francisco Goya c.1817, image in the public domain, accessed via Wikimedia Commons.

Cane Hill Asylum, postcard from the collection of Janet Few.

Chapter 9: The Romany and Traveller Community

Irish Travellers' Decorated Caravan. National Library of Ireland, accessed via Wikimedia Commons (6136023633). Also on the cover.

Gypsies Fortune Telling from the Robert Dawson Romani Collection, used under Creative Commons CC BY-SA 4.0, accessed via Wikimedia Commons.

Romany Vardo of the English Gypsies early twentieth century. Image in the public domain, accessed via Wikimedia Commons.

Chapter 10: Witchcraft

A Witch and a Devil making a Nail with which to make a Boy Lame, 1720. Wellcome Library, London, Wellcome Images V0025812EBL **http://wellcomeimages.org**, used under Creative Commons CC-BY-4.0.

Witches and Devils Dancing in a Circle, 1720. Wellcome Library, London, Wellcome Images V0025811ETR **http://wellcomeimages.org**, used under Creative Commons CC-BY-4.0.

Pricking for a Witch © Janet Few.

Chapter 11: Other Marginalised Groups

A Catalogue of the several Sects and Opinions in England and other Nations, Broadsheet 1647, British Museum. Image in the public domain.

Hannah Snell, John Faber. Image in the public domain, accessed via Wikimedia Commons.

The Tribunal 1919. Image in the public domain.

ACKNOWLEDGEMENTS

The name of a single author on the cover of a book masks the contribution of many people who played a part in its creation. I have been fortunate to have been helped by friends and colleagues along the way. It is always dangerous to name names for fear of offending those who might inadvertently be omitted, but this is a book about marginalisation, so it would be particularly inappropriate to marginalise those who have supported me by ignoring their involvement. I would like to thank all the members of the A Few Forgotten Women team, **https://afewforgottenwomen.wixsite.com/affw**, for their friendship, their generosity in sharing their expertise, their willingness to be beta readers and for allowing me, on occasions, to be a grumpy old woman. The encouragement of my writers' group has been also invaluable and has helped me to realise that all authors have times when writing becomes a millstone. I have to thank Dave Watson for alerting me to William Wilcox's story; Dai Davies of GenealCymru for the insightful sensitivity reading and Martha Barnard for the incredible initial proofreading and comments; any mistakes that remain are my own. Thanks too go to the helpful team at Pen & Sword for all their hard work. Finally, I pay tribute to my nearest and dearest for tolerating my absorption with this project.

INTRODUCTION

This book focuses on helping family historians with British ancestry to research those whose conditions or behaviours may have led them to become marginalised, or discriminated against. The categories that are covered here intersect; a single relative might, for example, be poor, illegitimate and sick; many of the marginalised were also criminalised.

The circumstances that led to individuals becoming marginalised were often the result of personal misfortune, exacerbated by society's attitudes. Many of those who are discussed in this book were victims of prejudice in the past because there was an intolerance of difference. Fear led to groups of people being stigmatised. This might have been a fear of social disorder, a fear of conflict, or a fear of an increased pressure on limited resources. There has been and sadly still is in some quarters, a tendency to victimise those who are 'not like us'. Often, it is our marginalised ancestors who have the most interesting stories to discover. We owe it to them to try to understand the society in which they lived and to bring them back from the margins, so that their lives are remembered.

The nature of this book means that it deals with subjects that make for uncomfortable reading. Searching for our ancestors in the records described in this book can at times be harrowing. In addition, sensitive issues can be raised, so the findings should be handled with care. Discovering a marginalised family member might spark very different reactions in their living relatives, ranging from excitement to embarrassment, which could lead to discord. The passage of time can affect opinions; instances that occurred several generations ago may be viewed as being fascinating, whereas discoveries about more recent ancestors could be regarded by some as shocking or shameful.

Attitudes towards certain actions and situations change over time, sometimes quite rapidly. There are those who we do not, in the twenty-first century, consider to be on society's margins, who would have been stigmatised in the not-too-distant past. Think about the Australian reaction to convict ancestry for example. Whereas this would once have been a source of shame, transported ancestors are now regarded as 'Australian royalty'. Within living memory, family instances of illegitimacy, mental illness, disability or homosexuality might well have been hushed up. Today we feel differently. Behaviour towards those from some racial or ethnic backgrounds has also changed over time.

Not all groups who were marginalised in the past have been included in this book; readers may identify other categories that could have been mentioned. Women have been sidelined in many spheres, but there is no chapter dedicated especially to them; you will notice, however, that many of the case studies focus on females. An absence from this book does not suggest that the discrimination and intolerance that these groups might have experienced has been ignored. I have had to be selective and can only apologise for marginalising the omitted groups in yet another way.

This book is not intended to be a complete guide to researching every individual topic. There are many other excellent publications that cover each subject in more depth. The intention here has been to provide some context, to outline the principal relevant sources and to set readers on the right path. The further reading suggests where more can be learned about the records and also the historical and societal background that led to the prejudice and discrimination experienced by some of our relatives.

This book raises many difficult issues. On occasions, I have quoted from contemporary documents and used terms in their context that are not acceptable today. This is the language of the past and it is important not to shy away from the fact that these words were commonly used, often with pejorative connotations. I fervently hope that I have not caused offence. Some of the most emotive sections of the book have been checked with the specific aim of ensuring that the phraseology was appropriate at the time of writing. If you are sharing family stories that cover issues such as disability, ethnicity or sexuality, especially if you are writing as someone from a different community, you may like to consider giving your text to a knowledgeable person for sensitivity reading, before making it more widely available.

Whilst we need to be mindful of the sensitivities of our living relatives and other readers when we tell our family's story, we do need to take an holistic approach and ensure that ancestors do not get disregarded just because their lives take us down a difficult path. If we, as genealogists, do not research the life histories of the victims of prejudice and preserve their memories, who will? This book is designed to encourage you to seek out the marginalised ancestors in your family and tell their stories.

I hope that you will accept the challenge. At the same time, there are ethical issues involved here. Would great-granny want the world to know that she was a criminal, a prostitute, or in an asylum? She was not a character in an historical novel but a real person, with her own sensibilities and feelings, that need to be respected. There is a fine balance between recording the lives of the people of the past and exposing our ancestors to the public gaze in a sensationalist manner. I believe that we need to try to understand our ancestors and that all their stories deserve to be told, even if this involves confronting challenging topics. What is crucial is that the accounts are handled in a sensitive and non-judgemental way and that the experiences of our ancestors are set within the context of their times.

Janet Few
Devon 2023

Chapter 1

POVERTY

Historically, those living in poverty were stigmatised and found themselves on society's margins. Particularly prior to the establishment of the welfare state, struggling to meet the expense of feeding, housing and clothing a family was an experience that was shared by many. An accident to the main breadwinner, a crop failure, or the collapse of a local industry, would have catastrophic effects. It is very difficult to gauge the extent of poverty in the past, as it varied with area and economic conditions. Individuals who were elderly, sick or widowed were more likely to face destitution than those who could earn a full wage.

At a time when travel and communications were difficult, much administration and government, including the provision for paupers, needed to be local. In the Medieval era, the responsibility for the poor lay with the manor but relief was usually undertaken by the church, through the monastic houses. The monasteries, nunneries and friaries provided doles of food and clothing, as well as medical treatment. These institutions might also administer private charitable trusts set up by individuals. This ended with the dissolution of the monasteries in 1536. Unfortunately, the removal of this provision coincided with an era of rapidly increasing population, a series of bad harvests and the collapse of the woollen industry in the face of foreign competition. The problem was compounded by significant inflation and the conversion of arable land to pasture, reducing the need for labourers. At the same time, the enclosure and redistribution of common land, a process that continued into the twentieth century, deprived labourers of traditional grazing rights. High levels of unemployment and vagrancy resulted in the evolution of a system of relief; this was created not out of compassion but stemmed from the fear of social unrest. Poverty was regarded as being entirely the result of the paupers' laziness and lack of effort.

There had been a number of Medieval statutes concerning beggars and the poor and there is evidence of church rates being levied in the fourteenth century. An act of 1531 acknowledged that there were differing causes of poverty. The infirm were given licences to beg and were obliged to wear a badge declaring their status. Those deemed to be lazy were whipped and returned to their native parish.

From the sixteenth century until 1834, the role of the parish in providing for the poor was key. In 1536, parishes were ordered to collect money to support those who were elderly or infirm, known as the impotent poor, so that they would not need to beg. By 1552, each parish was to appoint alms collectors, who sought voluntary contributions to aid the poor. This proved inadequate, so payments were made compulsory in 1563, and in 1572 the office of the overseer of the poor was officially created. Poor relief was extended to the able-bodied in 1576 but the paupers were expected to work in return for help. To facilitate this, non-residential workhouses were to be set up in each town and raw materials provided, so that paupers could undertake such tasks as spinning or weaving.

In the 1590s, former soldiers travelling home from the wars with Spain were given assistance to reach their own parishes but frequently arrived to find themselves homeless, lacking employment and without further support. They were often reduced to begging, contributing to an existing problem with vagrancy. In 1572, it had been ruled that all beggars were to be 'grievously whipped and burnt through the gristle of the right ear'. By 1597, the Act for the Repression of Vagrancy stated that vagrants should 'be stripped naked from the middle upwards and be openly whipped until his or her back be bloody'. They were then to be sent back to their birthplace or place of residence by a fixed route, being whipped at every deviation from it. They might also be taken to the House of Correction. In 1602, the baptism register of Heddington, Wiltshire records the baptism of John Allen, the son of John and Elener his wife with the note, 'the parents travelling homeward after they had been taken and whipped as sturdy beggars (according to the statute) was born here in the church house the 5th March being Easter Monday at night and baptised the next day'.

Those who were defined as vagrants, by the terms of the 1597 act, were a varied group of people including:

- Wandering scholars seeking alms.
- Shipwrecked seamen.
- Idle persons using subtle craft in games or in fortune telling.
- Pretended proctors, procurers or gatherers of alms for institutions.
- Fencers, bearwards, common players or minstrels.
- Jugglers, tinkers, peddlers and petty chapmen.

- Able-bodied wandering persons and labourers refusing to work for current rates of wages.
- Discharged pensioners.
- Wanderers pretending losses by fire.
- Egyptians or gypsies.

Later additions and amendments to the act added to the list 'idle and disorderly persons', those in possession of 'burgularious implements' and anyone dealing in unlicensed lottery tickets.

The Old, or Elizabethan, Poor Law was a significant piece of legislation. Originally passed in 1597/8 and ratified in 1601, it was to form the basis for relief of the poor for over 200 years. The act classified the poor in three ways. The infirm were to be institutionalised in parish poorhouses. The industrious poor would be given work in Houses of Correction but would not necessarily have to reside there. Idle vagabonds were to be whipped and returned to their native parish; a third vagabondage offence might be punishable by hanging.

The grandly named Act for Supplying some Defects in the Laws for the Relief of the Poor of this Kingdom, of 1697, attempted to tidy up the provisions of the Elizabethan Poor Law and reinforced the idea of requiring those receiving relief to be publicly identifiable. This measure was not retracted until 1810 but by then, may not have been rigorously enforced. All those receiving relief, including children, were to wear a badge on their right shoulder with the initial letter of their home parish, followed by a P. Paupers not displaying their badge ran the risk of a whipping or imprisonment, and overseers of the poor who were found providing relief to a pauper who was not 'badged' could be fined £1. The Churchwardens' Accounts for Harefield in Greater London refer to this practice in a series of entries. 'Pd for red cloath to make the pees and to John Hill for the making of them 1/9'. 'Paid John Hill taylor for 24 pees 4/0'. 'Spent when the poor had their pees set on 3/0'. 'Given to Spakman to give poor notice to wear pees 6d'.

Parishes funded poor relief by collecting from the more comfortably off citizens and using the money to support the parish's paupers and maintain the poorhouse. Paupers were rarely given money; instead, food, clothing, fuel or medical care would be provided. The account books of the overseers of the poor not only name the contributors to and recipients of parish poor relief but also refer to tradesmen and others whose services were used to help the poor. The accounts for 1762 for Brighstone on the Isle of Wight read:

For Coal for widow Low 10/6
For a sheet for Jean Leake 4/-

> For John Dore in the smallpox £2 11/-
> Lord's rent for the poor house 2/-
> For Woodford for faggots for Thomas Stephens 15/-
> For a Cloth Coat for Beak Thomson 4/-
> For Sebastien Thomson for shoes 8/9

Poor relief took two forms: out-relief, whereby the pauper received help but remained in their own home; and indoor relief, which necessitated being resident in the poorhouse or workhouse. Each parish was to provide a poorhouse in order to administer indoor relief. These were often little more than a cottage and might be used as both an institution for the infirm and the House of Correction. In fact, a Parliamentary Report of 1776/7, entitled an *Abstract of the Returns made by the Overseers of the Poor*, stated that there were about 2,000 parish poorhouses in England and Wales, suggesting that many parishes found other ways of managing their paupers.

Attitudes to poverty were exemplified by the Reverend Joseph Townsend's *Dissertation on the Poor Laws* written in 1785.

> The wisest legislator will never be able to devise a more equitable, a more effectual, or in any respect a more suitable punishment, than hunger is for the disobedient servant. Hunger will tame the fiercest animals; it will teach decency and civility, obedience and subjection, to the most brutish, the most obstinate, the most perverse. … Unless the degree of pressure be increased, the labouring poor will never acquire the habits of diligent application, and of severe frugality.
>   To increase this pressure, the poor tax must be gradually reduced in certain proportions annually, the sum to be raised in each parish being fixed and certain, not boundless and obliged to answer unlimited demands. This enormous tax might in the space of nine years be reduced nine-tenths; and the remainder being reserved as a permanent supply, the poor might safely be left to the bounty of the rich, without the interposition of any other law. But if the whole system of compulsive charity were abolished, it would be still better for the State.

George Nicholls, writing in the 1820s, said, 'I wish to see the Poor House looked to with dread by our labouring classes and the reproach for being an inmate of it extend downwards from father to son.' With widely held opinions such as these, it is not surprising that the main aim, when considering how to deal with the poor, was not the welfare of the paupers but minimising the financial outlay. In 1772/3, the Workhouse

Test Act, also known as the Knatchbull Act, attempted to reduce the numbers seeking help by requiring those receiving poor relief to enter the workhouse and be prepared to work.

It became apparent that money could be saved if parishes combined their efforts. As early as 1696, there were acts setting out local provision for specific towns, leading to the establishment of incorporated workhouses in larger towns and cities, whereby parishes could work together. Early examples in rural areas were in Suffolk, Norfolk and on the Isle of Wight. These incorporations were deemed to be successful, the measure of success being based solely on the cost. Building on this pattern, in 1782, Gilbert's Act encouraged partial amalgamations of parishes for the purposes of poor relief. About 100 such 'Gilbert Unions' had been established by 1834.

Following the recommendations of the 1832 report of the Poor Law Commission, a major change came in 1834, with the passing of the Poor Law Amendment Act, often called the New Poor Law. From this point, poor relief was controlled by Poor Law Unions, working under a Board of Guardians. Each town built a large workhouse, capable of housing hundreds of inmates, who were drawn from the town itself and its rural hinterland. Peter Higginbotham's website **www.workhouses.org.uk** is a key resource for information about workhouses. Here you will find plenty of background material describing the administration of the Poor Laws of both 1601 and 1834. There are details of many individual Union Workhouses; these include, pictures, location maps and the whereabouts of records. Amongst other things on this site, you will find information about some parish poorhouses, a workhouses timeline, accounts of life in the workhouse, a virtual workhouse museum and an explanation of the treatment of vagrants.

Workhouse records usually date from 1834–1948 and the most useful are the admissions' registers, listing all those entering and leaving the workhouse. There are also lists of those receiving out-relief, account books, minutes of the meetings of the Board of Guardians, staff records, birth and death records, apprenticeship records, creed registers detailing inmates' religious beliefs and lists of poor people's goods on entering the workhouse. These records are normally found in county or borough archives and as yet, only a very small number are available online.

The second half of the nineteenth century saw the spread of the ragged school system, designed to provide for destitute and vagrant children, many of whom were referred to the schools by the courts. The terms 'ragged school' and 'industrial school' were used interchangeably but a report in the *Leeds Mercury* of 5 December 1862, points out that industrial schools were founded to take children 'lower in the scale

Gressenhall Workhouse © Janet Few.

of society' than the ragged schools; in particular, catering for children under the age of 12, who had been referred by the courts following a first conviction. Ragged schools might also be licensed to take children from the courts, in addition to their other pupils. Accommodation was provided, so relatives may appear in the census return for one of these institutions.

The children at ragged and industrial schools were given a basic education and taught skills, such as laundry or carpentry, that might enable them to earn a living. Admissions' registers may survive in county archives, giving details of the child's circumstances, sometimes accompanied by a physical description; a few are available online. It is in the registers for the Leeds Industrial School, that we find Isabella Hutton, who was in trouble for 'consorting with thieves', having been abandoned by her mother in a Liverpool workhouse and 8-year-old Anne Mary Fletcher who was left destitute after the death of her mother. Their contemporary, Louisa McDermott, is described in the records as being of stout build, with blue eyes, brown hair and freckles. In 1866, at the age of 13, she was sent out begging to support her three younger sisters; all four girls were placed in the industrial school.

In 1861, a census was taken of all those who had been continuously resident in a workhouse for at least five years. This is arranged by

Poor Law Union and lists over 14,000 paupers, giving details of length of stay and the reason for the pauper being in an institution. Images are available on Ancestry **www.ancestry.co.uk** and Findmypast **www.findmypast.co.uk**.

Private charities continued to help the poor and records of the administration of these, perhaps with details of recipients of help, may be in county archives, estate archives, private hands or with a local church, who might have been appointed to administer the charity. References to bequests for the poor might be found in wills.

Vagrants, known as 'the houseless poor', continued to be a source of concern into the nineteenth century. The 1824 Vagrants' Act is, with some modifications, still on the statute books. This defined 'idle and disorderly persons' as follows:

- Every person wandering abroad and lodging in any barn or outhouse, or in any deserted or unoccupied building, or in the open air, or under a tent, or in any cart or waggon, not having any visible means of subsistence and not giving a good account of himself or herself.
- Every person wilfully exposing to view, in any street, road, highway, or public place, any obscene print, picture, or other indecent exhibition.
- Every person wandering abroad, and endeavouring by the exposure of wounds or deformities to obtain or gather alms.
- Every person going about as a gatherer or collector of alms, or endeavouring to procure charitable contributions of any nature or kind, under any false or fraudulent pretence.

After 1834, casual wards, sometimes known as spikes, provided basic shelter for destitute itinerants and vagrants, in return for work, such as picking oakum or crushing stones until they were small enough to fit through a grill. Although these might be attached to a workhouse, the provision in a vagrants' ward differed from that of a workhouse. Workhouses were designed for those who lived within its catchment area, whereas anyone could seek refuge at a casual ward. It was thought prudent to keep the vagrants separate from the workhouse inmates for fear of infection. Those in the casual wards might be locked in a cell until the requisite amount of work had been completed to compensate for the cost of their stay. Some records of those admitted to vagrants' wards survive in local archives.

The urban homeless who had managed to earn a few pence might pay a penny or two for shelter in a common lodging house, or dosshouse. If they could not afford a bed they would take the cheaper alternative

Applicants for Admission to a Casual Ward, *Sir Luke Fildes. Tate Gallery Image released under Creative Commons CC-BY-NC-ND (3.0 Unported).*

and sleep hanging over a rope; possibly giving rise to the expressions 'hungover' and 'on the ropes'.

The responsibility for providing poor relief was rooted in the principle of belonging. Parishes, and later workhouses, only had to provide for those who were deemed to be settled in their area. Those who contributed to the parish poor rates, which would have been all but the poorest residents, were keen to keep their payments low and would not want to increase their responsibilities by allowing additional people to become settled in their parish. For this reason, apart from marriage, the conditions under which a new settlement could be acquired were designed so that it was unlikely that anyone in a potentially precarious financial state could change their settlement.

At its simplest, an individual's parish of settlement was their birthplace. In 1662, the Act of Settlement set out the conditions under which a person could change their parish of settlement. Women took their husband's parish of settlement on marriage and kept it into widowhood. This might result in a needy widow being sent across the country to a place of settlement that she had never visited. Renting property worth £10 a year, paying parish or poor rates, or serving as a parish official, gave an individual settlement in that parish. Working for at least a year under a settled master, or completing an apprenticeship in the parish also conferred settled status. Unsettled people residing in a parish were 'sojourners' and this is a term often seen in marriage registers. They may have lived in the parish for a number of years

A Glasgow Slum, *Thomas Annan 1861 British Library. Image in the public domain, accessed via Wikimedia Commons.*

without qualifying for settlement. Settlement legislation remained in force until 1876.

A newcomer to the parish would be examined within forty days of arrival and questioned as to their place of birth, previous abodes and employment history. At first, it was possible to lie low until the forty days had expired, after which the authorities could do nothing, so, in 1685, an amendment to the 1662 act ruled that the forty days only began when the individual declared themself to the overseer; later, new arrivals would be announced in church.

On 13 April 1846, Mary Ann Smith, then residing in Cerne Union Workhouse in Dorset, was examined saying:

> My maiden name was Mary Ann Diskell. I married my late deceased husband William Smith at the parish church of East Compton in the said county on the tenth day of November six years last November. I have by my said husband two children, Thomas Smith aged three years and Frank Smith aged two years and upward. My husband died about 16 weeks since. I am now with my said two children in the care of the Union Workhouse and chargeable to the Parish of Callistock.

Interestingly, her father-in-law, John Smith, was examined on the same day and a much lengthier examination survives for him.

If new arrivals, who appeared to lack any means of supporting themselves, or an individual seeking relief, was found to belong to another area, a removal order would be issued by the Justices of the Peace, ordering the incomer back to their parish of settlement. They would be escorted by the parish constable to the parish boundary and handed over to the constable of the next parish until they finally reached their destination. This might cost a parish far more than helping the person where they were, but the principle of only assisting their own held strong. For example, in 1760, the overseers of St Leonard's, Shoreditch in London, sought to remove George Wood, his wife and three children back to Culmstock in Devon, a distance of 170 miles.

From 1743/4, it was normal for children under the age of 7 to remain with their mothers but on 21 February 1810, the parish of Shoreditch ordered the removal of Sarah Ann, the 4-year-old illegitimate child of Ann Glasscock, formerly Grant. The child was to be sent back to the London parish of St Thomas's, Queen Street. Ann Glasscock had been examined 'touching her settlement previous to marriage and as to the settlement of her illegitimate child'. The examination reveals that Ann, at the age of 12, had gone to work for Joseph Rainbow in St Thomas's and was paid £6 a year for the first two years, her wages raising to £8 after that. She remained there for three years and three months, not subsequently gaining any settlement elsewhere. The record also states that Ann married Thomas Glasscock in 1807, at St Martin in the Fields, London.

According to the examination, Ann's daughter, Sarah Ann, had been born on 22 December 1805 in Westminster Lying-in Hospital in Lambeth. Ann named the father in the examination as Thomas Chitham Keynock of 4 Canterbury Court, St Andrew's Hill. A settlement examination is perhaps not the most obvious place to seek the name of the father of an illegitimate child. Sarah Ann is recorded, in the baptism register of St Mary's Lambeth, as being baptised on the same day as her birth; no father is named.

Apart from the settlement examinations and removal orders, from 1696/7 settlement legislation also gave rise to settlement bonds and settlement certificates. Settlement bonds were signed promises by an individual, pledging to support a named newcomer should they need poor relief. If a parishioner wanted to move to a new area to seek work, their parish of settlement would issue a certificate, acknowledging their responsibility should the person need help in the future. This gave the new parish reassurance and would ensure that the migrants were given the opportunity to settle in a different area without being precipitately removed. There would have been two copies of the certificate, one would have been kept in the issuing parish and the other given to the traveller. This copy may then have found its way into the parish chest of the new abode. In 1756, a settlement certificate was issued by the overseers of the poor for Fontmell Magna, Dorset, acknowledging their responsibility for William and Mary Haine, their son William and their three daughters, Nanny, Betty and Lucy, who wished to move to Blandford Forum; this is now with the records for Blandford Forum.

Records relating to settlement and removal, as well as the records of the overseers of the poor, are part of what are termed 'parish chest' documents, as they would have been kept, along with the parish registers, in the locked chest that each parish was expected to provide. Disputes sometimes occurred between parishes, regarding the responsibility for paupers and these might be heard in the Quarter Sessions Courts; in this case, references would appear in their records and perhaps be reported in the press. Surviving settlement documents will almost certainly be in county archives, with only a few starting to be digitised and made available online. Unfortunately, many of the documents have been lost and to find anything for the seventeenth century is rare.

The most efficient way to abrogate responsibility for a pauper was to send them overseas. There were child emigration schemes, paying for children to start a new life abroad, in operation from 1618–1967. Both government and private assisted passage schemes for adults and children reached a peak between 1850 and 1920. There are relevant records at The National Archives **www.nationalarchives.gov.uk;** in particular, Poor Law Union papers relating to pauper emigration can be found in class MH12. Private charities also maintained their own records.

It is important to acknowledge that most of us have ancestors who would have been familiar with the hardship that accompanied living on a low, uncertain, or non-existent income. The poor were often blamed and despised for their condition, which was seen as being of their own making. The stigma of poverty was an additional burden for those who were already struggling to feed, clothe and house themselves and their families.

The Story of Harriet Bentlif

On 8 December 1835, Harriet Bentlif was examined regarding her place of legal settlement by St Luke's parish, Chelsea in London. Harriet stated that she had never been married. She had worked for two years as a servant for Mr Baker, a linen draper of Upper Eaton Street, Pimlico, but had left four years earlier and had done nothing to gain settlement elsewhere since. The settlement examination stated that Harriet was pregnant and chargeable to Lambeth in Surrey. An accompanying removal order shows that Harriet was sent back to Lambeth. No other record of this child has been found; perhaps Harriet experienced a stillbirth.

Harriet appears in the workhouse records for Christ Church workhouse in Southwark in 1847, having been sent there by order from Rotherhithe. She was described as being an able-bodied, single needlewoman. With her were three of her illegitimate children, George born in 1838, Charles, born two years later and Edward born in 1843.

Harriet came from a non-conformist family. Her birth, together with that of four of her siblings, was registered, on 30 June 1837, in the General Register of Protestant Dissenters, sometimes called Doctor Williams' Register. It is probably no coincidence that this was the day before civil registration came into force. According to the registers, Harriet had been born on 15 December 1813 in Gravesend, Kent. Registered on the same day were her older sister Sarah Godfrey Bentlif, born in 1811 and younger sister Amelia, born in 1815, also in Gravesend. The registrations for Harriet's two brothers, which also took place on 30 June, show that, by the time of their births in 1821 and 1824, the family were living at 41 Long Lane, Bermondsey, London. *The London Gazette* and other press reports, suggest a likely reason for the move. Their father, David, a Gravesend shoemaker, was declared bankrupt in 1818 and spent time in the Fleet debtors' prison.

In 1843, a David Bentliff [sic] was tried for larceny in the Old Bailey and was found not guilty. This may have been Harriet's father or brother. A George Bentliff, almost certainly Harriet's brother, also found himself on the wrong side of the law. The *London Evening Standard* of 8 March 1847 reveals that George was found guilty of stealing bread and cheese from a wagon in Kensington. Having been previously transported, he was once again sentenced to transportation. He left for New South Wales on the *Hashemy*.

In 1851, Harriet, an unmarried charwoman, was living in part of 93 Great Suffolk Street in Southwark; she was enumerated as Bentley. With her were two 'nephews' Charles and Edward Maynard. Charles's birthplace and age suggest that he was in fact Harriet's son. Edward was born in 1847 in Rotherhithe and registered as Maynard, with the mother's maiden name Bentlif. Was he the second son that Harriet had had named Edward, or was his age incorrectly recorded in the workhouse record? It seems that perhaps Harriet had been living as if she was the wife of a Mr Maynard.

Ten years later, Harriet 'Bentley', now claiming to be a widow, was living at 7 Brewer's Court in Bermondsey, working as a monthly nurse; a George Maynard 'son', was with her. Again, the age and birthplace for George is consistent with that for George Bentlif in the workhouse admissions' register. Harriet Bentlif, of 7 Heeton's Place, Bermondsey, was buried in Tower Hamlets Cemetery on 30 September 1878.

Chapter 2

CRIMINALITY

Sometimes, the criminals in our family are those we come to know best, which is what makes searching for them so rewarding. Records might include detailed physical descriptions and photographs. For example, John Grantham, of Sherbourne, Dorset, was admitted to Gloucester County Gaol in 1867. He was 5ft 6in tall, with hazel eyes, an oval face and fresh complexion, his dark hair was turning grey. The register of prisoners reveals that John had a hare lip, a cast in his left eye, a scar on the back of his neck and the joint of his fourth left finger was enlarged. Discovering that an ancestor was convicted of a crime might explain why a family's circumstances changed, or account for a large gap in the family's children.

Several of the categories of marginalised ancestor that are discussed in this book might have found themselves caught up in the criminal justice system. Sometimes they were innocent, sometimes they acted out of malice, but often they were driven to commit a crime by poverty and desperation. It is interesting to consider our reactions to discovering criminal ancestors. Does finding a child abuser in the family provoke an emotion that is different from the impact of finding a smuggler, who might be considered romantic? It is important to set this within the context of the time; historically, the smuggler would have been given the harsher sentence. We might feel affection for the lawbreakers in our family but society viewed them very differently.

Criminality created a range of documentation, with many surviving records. One of the first places to seek evidence of criminals is in the newspaper archives, as most cases were reported in the press, often quite fully. The reports can point towards the original court or prison records, where first-hand evidence might be found. The British Newspaper Archive is available at **www.britishnewspaperarchive.co.uk** and can also be accessed via Findmypast **www.findmypast.co.uk**. *The Bedfordshire*

Mercury of 21 October 1893 stated that 52-year-old labourer, George Braybrooke, was charged with stealing a live duck, worth 2s 6d, from Francis Charles Wright, and a pair of child's socks from John Bowskill. Although Braybrooke claimed he had bought the duck from a butcher, the bird was identified from its head and feet by the owner. On being found guilty, Braybrooke admitted that he had served nine months in jail for a felony in 1885. 'The Chairman in his sentencing said there was a page and a half of previous convictions against the prisoner, who had suffered every kind of imprisonment from five years penal servitude, as he admitted and he would now go to prison for twelve months hard labour.'

The Criminal Registers are a key source. They are held in classes HO26 and HO27 at The National Archives **www.nationalarchives.gov.uk** and are available on both Ancestry and Findmypast. Class HO26 lists all those in Middlesex who were charged with indictable offences between 1787 and 1850. After this date, the Middlesex records are included in HO27. HO27 covers the period 1805–1892 for the whole of England and Wales, with Middlesex from 1850 onwards. The registers are arranged by county and give the offender's name, crime, sentence and whether or not they were acquitted or discharged. They reveal that, at Guildford Assizes of August 1862, Charles Rawson was accused of maliciously firing a haystack. He was found not guilty on the grounds of insanity and was to be 'kept in strict custody'.

How would our ancestors have been tried? By the later Middle Ages, the system of trial by ordeal had been superseded by an evidence-based, inquisitorial system, where statements were collected and witnesses cross-examined. The slightly different procedures that applied in cases involving witchcraft are discussed in Chapter 10. In England and Wales, from the late fifteenth century until 1875, a hierarchy of civil courts dealt with criminal cases. In addition, trials for some crimes took place in ecclesiastical and manorial courts.

At the bottom of the civil court ladder were the Petty Sessions, which were held in most towns every few weeks and might meet in a local inn. They could only deal with minor offences, so many cases were referred to the Quarter Sessions Courts. These met, as the name suggests, four times a year in each county, with the exception of Middlesex, where they only met twice a year. Justices of the Peace presided over both the Petty and Quarter Sessions. The records for these courts are held in county archives. Dalton's manual for Justices of the Peace, *A Countrey* [sic] *Justice*, published in 1618, emphasised the need to seek information on the character and family of all suspected felons. He advised the justices to investigate:

> his parents, if they were wicked … His nature, if civill or hastie, wittie or subtle, a quarreller, pilferer, or bloudie minded …

His trade; for if a man liveth idly or vagrant … it is good cause to arrest him on suspicion … His companie … His course of life; if a common alehouse haunter, or riotous in dyet, play or apparrell. Whether he be of evil fame or report.

More serious cases were referred to the Assizes Courts; itinerant judges visited county towns twice a year to hear these cases. The National Archives holds the records in classes beginning ASSI; they include calendars of prisoners and indictments. Indictments may give the accused's name, abode, age, marital status, date and nature of the alleged offence, verdict and details of the victim. Statements taken from witnesses prior to a trial, known as depositions, have not survived well. County archives might have lists of those to be tried at the Assizes, known as Assize Calendars. The National Archives has a number of useful research guides relating to court and criminal records, including *Criminal Court Cases: assize courts 1559–1971*, available to download from their website.

The central London courts, such as the Court of King's (or Queen's) Bench and until 1642, the Court of Star Chamber, also heard cases, as did the Central Criminal Court, better known as The Old Bailey. Old Bailey Online, a free database of nearly 200,000 trials that were heard by the Central Criminal Court between 1674 and 1913, is available at **www.oldbaileyonline.org**. Searches can be made for the names of the accused, the victim, the witnesses and the arresting officers. One such case, heard in 1693, involved William Read, 'a Countrey Fellow, who came from Taunton in the West'. He was tried for stealing eighteen weather-sheep, valued at 30 shillings each, from Mr William Sympson, 'who said, that he lost the Sheep out of Ham Marshes in Middlesex, and the Sheep were found in the custody of the Prisoner. The Prisoner said, that one Thomas Williams hired him to drive the Sheep to London, but could not produce Williams to prove it.' He was found guilty; no details of his punishment are given.

Some civil cases were, until 1875, heard in the Court of Common Pleas, whose records are in classes beginning with CP at The National Archives. Disputes over inheritance, marriage settlements, debts and land were held in the Court of Chancery and the Court of Exchequer, whose records are also at The National Archives.

Between 1876 and 1971, the court system was broadly similar to that of preceding centuries, but the central courts were brought together as the Supreme Court of Judicature, which included a High Court and a Court of Appeal.

In 1972, the Crown Court system was introduced. From this time, Magistrates' Courts heard the vast majority of cases, with more serious crimes being tried in the Crown Courts. Both Crown and Magistrates' Courts keep records of more recent cases. Some Magistrates' Court records can be found in county and city archives. Most Crown Court records that are more than 25 to 30 years old are deposited with The National Archives.

The Court Baron, a manorial court that met every three or four weeks, also heard cases within the jurisdiction of the lord of the manor. These might involve disputes over land tenure, slander, libel, or civil matters such as diverting a water course or leaving a dunghill in the wrong place. Up until 1732, the records are normally in Latin. The Manorial Documents Register, accessible on The National Archives website **https://discovery.nationalarchives.gov.uk/manor-search**, gives information about the survival and whereabouts of manorial documents.

The ecclesiastical courts of the archbishops, bishops and archdeacons were at their height from the middle of the fifteenth century until the middle of the seventeenth century. They primarily heard cases of a religious and moral nature, such as blasphemy, heresy, apostasy, fornication and adultery. Presumed witches might also be tried in the ecclesiastical courts. The records, again usually in Latin until 1732, are held in diocesan record offices and kept with the county archives. The York diocesan archive is at The Borthwick Institute **https://borthcat.york.ac.uk** and that for Canterbury is at Lambeth Palace Library **www.lambethpalacelibrary.org**.

In Scotland, the lower courts, trying less serious crimes, were the Sheriff's Courts. The records are at National Records of Scotland **www.nrscotland.gov.uk** but are not fully indexed. In order to search them, you will need to find out which court heard the case from other sources, such as the newspapers. Appeals from the Sheriff's Courts and more serious cases, were heard in the High Court of Justiciary. National Records of Scotland holds the records of the High Court from 1790; there is a 100-year closure rule on these documents. Local Scottish archives may also have relevant records relating to Scottish criminals, such as police records.

Scotland's Court and Criminal Database 1708–1909 includes prison records, High Court trial papers and witness statements, known as Crown Office Precognitions. The Database can be searched on Scottish Indexes **www.scottishindexes.com/ScotlandsCriminalDatabase.aspx**. Here we learn that, in 1854, 25-year-old Alexander Herring alias John Stratford, a cattle drover, and 33-year-old Charles Hill, a flesher, both from Grassmarket, stole cattle from sheds near the Union Canal in Edinburgh. The cattle were the property of Andrew Oliphant of Strathmiglo, Fife and John Swan of Archibald Place in Edinburgh.

Punishments, for those who were convicted, evolved over time. In the sixteenth and seventeenth centuries, many punishments were based on public humiliation. The stocks and the pillory served as both a degrading experience for the offender and a deterrent for others. Public humiliation was also used by the church. The ecclesiastical courts often imposed public penance on those who were found guilty. This was particularly likely if the crimes were of a sexual nature, such as adultery,

William Prynne in the Pillory, *John Cassell 1865. Image in the public domain, accessed via Wikimedia Commons.*

fornication, or having an illegitimate child. In these instances, women were habitually punished more severely than men. Apostasy, the abandoning of the prevailing religious doctrines, was also punishable by public penance.

Penance took place during the Sunday church service at the penitence stone, which was usually by the church door, or those found guilty would have to prostrate themselves before the font. They might be expected to dress in sackcloth and ashes or a white shift. A confession, followed by a promise to reform, was expected. In 1635, Archbishop Laud and Dr Joseph Hall, Bishop of Exeter, published an official form of penance and reconciliation:

> He is to stand at all time of divine service and sermon in the forenoon in the porch of the church … in a penitent fashion in a white sheet, with a white wand in his hand, his head uncovered, his countenance dejected, not taking any particular notice of any person that passeth by him; and when the people come in and go out of the church, let him upon his knees humbly crave their prayers and acknowledge his offence in this form, 'Good Christians, remember in your prayers this poor apostate or renegado'.

In the seventeenth century, fuelled by fear, poverty and a rising population, alongside political and religious upheaval, attitudes to crime were changing. Increased literacy and the ease with which broadsheets, giving details of crimes, could be printed, led to the perception that crime was on the increase, which, per head of population, was not actually the case.

Punishments became increasingly severe during the eighteenth century, with the gradual introduction of laws that became known as The Bloody Code. Physical punishments such as whipping were common. In 1688, fifty different crimes attracted the death penalty. One hundred years later, the number had increased threefold. Until they were banned in 1868, public executions were a macabre form of entertainment, attracting spectators from the surrounding area. Following public pressure and some controversial cases, notably the executions of Timothy Evans, Derek Bentley and Ruth Ellis, the death penalty was abolished in Britain in 1969; the last execution having taken place in 1964. Northern Ireland followed suit in 1973. The exception was in cases of treason and although the final execution for treason was in 1946, the option for imposing the death penalty for this offence remained on the statute books until 1998.

In the past, those convicted of a capital crime could mitigate their sentence by claiming Benefit of the Clergy. This involved proving a level

Ducking a Scold, *an illustration from an eighteenth-century chap-book reproduced in* Chap-books of the eighteenth century, *John Ashton 1834. Image in the public domain, accessed via Wikimedia Commons.*

of literacy by reading what was known as 'The Neck Verse' from Psalm 51 verses 1–4. As the same passage was always used, it was possible to learn this by rote and thus give the impression of being able to read. Although the ability to claim Benefit of the Clergy was not revoked until 1827, its use dwindled from the end of the seventeenth century.

If a pregnant woman was sentenced to death, the punishment could not be carried out as the unborn child would also be killed. She could, therefore, 'plead her belly' and undergo an examination. She would need to be far enough advanced in her pregnancy for foetal movements to be detected. In theory, she would be returned to jail to give birth and her sentence would be carried out afterwards but sometimes this led to a reprieve, as a motherless child would become a financial burden on the parish. In 1720, Hannah Connor and Elizabeth Shanks, along with two male accomplices, were sentenced to death for the murder of Lieutenant Bicknell. The two women pleaded their bellies and were found to be pregnant, so their sentence was deferred.

With the exception of debtors, prison sentences were rarely handed out in the seventeenth century; parish lock-ups or bridewells tended to be used to hold those awaiting trial. Prison as a punishment in its own right was more frequently used from the later eighteenth century. Men, women and children were incarcerated together. Conditions in prisons

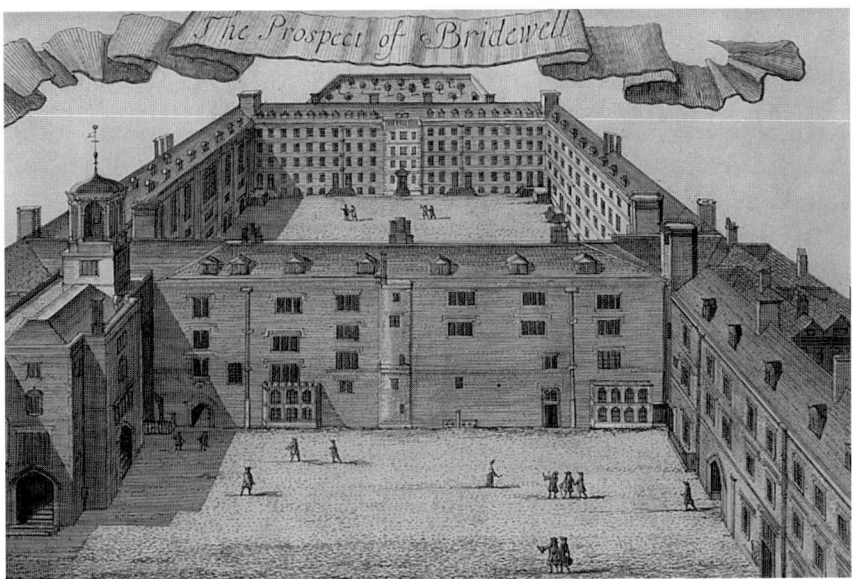

The Prospect of Bridewell, *from John Strype's* An Accurate Edition of Stow's Survey of London *1720. Image in the public domain, accessed via Wikimedia Commons.*

were poor, especially for those who lacked the money to ease their situation. Better food, fuel and the right to visitors, or the use of writing materials, was dependent on the ability to pay the gaoler. Sentences often included hard labour. Prisoners might be put to work crushing rock for the roads or picking oakum, stripping the tar from old rope. Prisoners were also given pointless tasks such as turning the 'screw', a crank handle, continuously, or walking on a treadmill.

In 1777, John Howard surveyed English and Welsh prisons and wrote a book entitled *The State of Prisons in England and Wales*. This spearheaded a campaign in some quarters to improve prison conditions. In 1813, Elizabeth Fry, the Quaker reformer, began her work in Newgate prison and life for prisoners gradually got better. Despite this, there was little public sympathy for criminals, who remained on the margins of society. Darwin's theory of natural selection, published in 1859, led to the idea that criminals were a sub-class of humans, who had not fully evolved and who could be identified by their appearance. Information about prison conditions and administration, as well as details of individual prisons can be found on Peter Higginbotham's website The Prison: the story of an institution **http://theprison.org.uk**.

Changes to methods of punishment came in the nineteenth century, with a reversal of the number of offences that were punishable by death. From this time, only murder and treason led to execution. The 1800s also saw the development of industrial and ragged schools, to which young

Cell with Prisoner at Crank-Labour in the Surrey House of Correction 1851, *from* London Labour and the London Poor, *Henry Mayhew 1851. Image in the public domain, accessed via Wikimedia Commons.*

offenders were referred; their role was discussed in the previous chapter. Policing too developed in the nineteenth century, with watchmen and elected parish constables being replaced by a professional, paid police force. The Metropolitan Police Force was created in 1829, with county forces following suit, until, by 1856, all towns and counties were obliged to set up a force.

There are several other classes of record at The National Archives that are useful when tracing criminal ancestors. These include the Calendars of Prisoners in HO140, which date from 1868 to 1929 and are available on Ancestry and Findmypast. They cover all those tried at Quarter Sessions and Assize Courts in England, Wales, the Isle of Man and the Channel Islands. Prisoners awaiting trial at the Central Criminal Court are also listed. The details include the date of admission to prison, name, occupation, age, level of education, details of the offence and victim, the name of the presiding judge, verdict and the sentence. For example, on 29 July 1884, in Leeds, Yorkshire, Eli Kershaw, a 30-year-old, illiterate collier was found guilty of 'feloniously assaulting' Sarah Smith and stealing a purse containing 1 shilling, the property of William Smith. The offence took place at Scawsby on 15 May 1884 and he was taken into custody two days later. Eli had previously received a sentence of six months for the aggravated assault of a female in 1882. He pleaded guilty to robbery with personal violence and was sentenced to fifteen months in Leeds prison; the names of the judge and the committing magistrates are also given. The registers for the Central Criminal Court for the period 1855–1931, with records of 78,000 individuals, contain similar information and are in class CRIM9; these are also available on Ancestry and Findmypast.

The Metropolitan Police's Habitual Criminals' Registers for 1881–1936 are in class MEPO6 at the National Archives and are available on Findmypast. These were circulated to police stations and list over 150,000 habitual criminals, stating whether or not the individual had been apprehended. Details include name, aliases, physical description, date and place of birth, marital status, place of last offence, length of sentence and period of police supervision, dates of conviction and liberation, prison from where liberated and destination on discharge. Within this class of records are the habitual drunkards' lists, which cover the period 1903–1914 and include photographs of the individuals. These were distributed to licensed premises each week, warning the landlords who to avoid serving.

There is a wealth of detail in the Home Office and Police Commission records. Those for 1770–1951, in class PCOM2 at the National Archives, are wide ranging, including calendars of prisoners, staff journals, habitual criminals' lists for English and Welsh prisons, for Gibraltar prison and for those on prison hulks, ships that held felons when there was insufficient space in prison. Some of the later records include photographs. Class PCOM3 contains records of male prisoners who were granted licences, allowing them to leave jail on parole. They date from 1853–1887 and include references to 45,535 individuals. The records include the prisoner's name and aliases, age, marital status, number of children, name and address of next of the kin, occupation, religion, whether they could read and write, crime, sentence, date and place of conviction and physical description; there are also photographs. In addition, you might find information about who the prisoner corresponded with, visits received whilst in prison and medical details. They also state where the prisoner was to live on release. Newgate Prison Registers in class HO77 at The National Archives are also on Findmypast.

Daniel Geary was listed in the Wandsworth Prison Registers in PCOM2, having been convicted on 3 April 1865 of dressing in his own clothes whilst in the workhouse. He was 40 years old, 5ft 5in tall with brown hair and blue eyes and had been born in England. He had a scar on his left cheek, was illiterate and had two previous convictions.

Criminal petitions for the period 1819–1853 are held in classes HO17 and HO18 at The National Archives and registers of criminal petitions for 1797–1853 are in class HO19. These are available on Findmypast. The records were generated when a criminal, or someone acting on their behalf, petitioned for a sentence to be reduced or overturned. There are also some petitions from prison governors recommending early release on the grounds of good behaviour; sometimes supporting evidence is included. The registers in HO19 may refer to appeals where other evidence no longer survives. Class HO47 at The National Archives, which is also available on Findmypast, contains reports by trial judges on cases dating from 1784–1830. These are appeals for the commutation of a sentence or a free pardon.

It is beyond the scope of this book to consider transportation in any detail but of course, it was the sentence for serious crimes. Seventy per cent of those convicted at The Old Bailey between 1718 and 1769 were transported. Transportation to North America and the West Indies began in 1615. Those reprieved following a death sentence were transported for fourteen years, with seven-year sentences for less serious crimes. In 1662, the Habeus Corpus Act limited the length of time that people could be held in prison without appearing in court. It also made exile illegal. Instead of banishment, a pardon could be given, conditional upon them leaving the country for a specified number of years. Their journeys were not made on the transport ships that are associated with later transportation to Australia. Under this scheme, prisoners were purchased from the sheriff by merchants. The money was used to pay the gaoler, the court and the clerk for drawing up a pardon. The criminals travelled on merchant ships. On arrival, the merchant sold the offender as an indentured servant, hoping to make a profit. It was, therefore, in their interest to keep the transportee healthy. The elderly and unfit were not a good investment, so ended up being held indefinitely awaiting transportation.

As the seventeenth century progressed, some colonies began to prohibit the importation of convicts under this scheme, with Virginia doing so in 1670, followed by Maryland in 1676 and Jamaica banning female convicts in 1697. In 1787, the first fleet sailed to Australia. This was different in nature from transportation across the Atlantic and conditions on the transport ships were harsh, with many transportees dying during the journey. The transportation registers from 1787 to 1870 are at The National Archives in class HO11 and images are available on Findmypast. The State Library of Queensland has compiled a database using these registers **www.digitalpanopticon.org/British_Transportation_Registers_1787–1867**.

Class HO8 at The National Archives contains over a million records of returns of prisoners held on hulks between 1782 and 1871; these are accessible at Findmypast. The lists were compiled each quarter and give information including name, age, offence, date and place of the offence, sentence, state of health, behaviour, and remarks, such as transported, died, or pardoned and the date. James Skinner aged 21, was held on board the aptly named *Retribution* at Sheerness, Kent, in June 1832. Accused of stealing an ass, he was convicted at Maidstone on 15 July 1830 and sentenced to seven years. He was suffering from scrofula and his behaviour was good. Class ADM6/418-422, at The National Archives and available on Findmypast, contains additional registers of convicts on some prison hulks for the period 1818–1831. The National Archives also holds records for the Metropolitan Police and the Royal Irish Constabulary. Other police records are held by the forces themselves or are in county archives.

This is not a complete list of the many records that might be used to trace criminal ancestors. More comprehensive advice can be found in books dedicated to the subject; there are some suggestions in the list of further reading. For up-to-date information on what is available online, look at The National Archives' Discovery catalogue; also go to Ancestry's Card Catalogue and Findmypast's 'All Record Sets' and search individually for 'Court', 'Criminal' and 'Prison'.

The Story of Frederick Michael Railton

Frederick Michael Railton was born in 1846 in Blackburn, Lancashire, the eldest child of John and Alice Railton née Polding. He grew up in a middle-class family in Pleasington, Blackburn, where his father was an engineer. By 1871, Frederick's father, John, was a land surveyor and local magistrate and Frederick, who was still living with his father, was a land valuer. John died in 1875 and within a few weeks, Frederick married Margaret Green in the parish church of Bolton-le-Moors. John had been the agent for the Phoenix Fire and Assurance Company and Frederick took over this role on his father's death.

Between January and July 1876, Frederick committed three acts of fraud. It seems that this went undetected for six months. On the 23 January 1877, a legal notice was issued by Phoenix Assurance and was reported in the press. It stated that they had cancelled the appointment of Frederick Michael Railton of 17 Broomfield Terrace, Witton but lately of 41 King Street, Blackburn, as land agent for the company and that he no longer acted for, or represented, them. Just one week later, Frederick's son, Ernest John, was born.

The newspapers reveal the circumstances behind Phoenix Assurance's declaration. Frederick appeared before the Blackburn magistrates, charged with forging acquittances in the company's name and thereby defrauding Messrs Hornby of £73 15s 9d and Messers Stones and Railton of £23 6s. The latter is particularly interesting, as presumably there was a family connection. There was also another forgery for £73.

The Calendar of Prisoners, in class HO140, describes Frederick's crimes as follows:

> Having at Blackburn on the 7 July 1876, feloniously forged a certain acquittance and receipt for money and entered the same with intent to defraud and having obtained from one John Gornall the sum of £15 17s 3d the property of James Bradley Stones and others with intent to defraud. He is also charged with having at Blackburn on the 7 April 1876 feloniously forged a certain acquittance and receipt for money and uttered the same with intent to defraud. He is further charged with having at Blackburn on the 6 January 1876 feloniously forged a certain acquittance and receipt for money and uttered the same with intent to defraud.

Blackburn police believed that Frederick had escaped to California, but Glasgow police continued the search, perhaps incentivised by the offer of a £25 reward. Frederick was duly apprehended on 17 February by the police in Glasgow and was found to have a ticket for the tender *Ethiopia* in his pocket. The *Ethiopia* transported passengers to larger sea-going vessels. A passage to America had been booked in the name of George F. Rostrons and when questioned, Frederick admitted that this was him.

The magistrates in Blackburn referred the case to the Liverpool Assizes, where Frederick pleaded guilty to three charges of forgery and was sentenced to seven years' penal servitude. The press made much of the fact that Frederick's late father had been a magistrate. The newspapers also reported that Frederick had set up an 'extravagant establishment' upon marriage and that he also 'had a habit of spending money freely in public houses'. Was Frederick planning on sending for his wife and child if he managed to establish himself in America, or was he attempting to shirk his responsibilities?

A range of criminal records give further information about Frederick, the most informative of which is his multi-page entry in the series of Home Office and Prison Commission Male Licences, in class PCOM3 at The National Archives and available via Findmypast. Frederick's record includes a photograph and medical history. From this, we learn that Frederick was a surveyor, his conduct and health were good and that he could read and write well. He had a dark complexion, brown eyes and brown hair, which was turning grey by the time of his release, at the age of 35. He was 5ft 4¼in tall and of stout build. He presumably lost weight in prison as his build was 'proportionate' on release. At the time of his conviction he was 30 years old and his last place of residence was Witton.

Frederick spent time in several prisons; initially he was at Kirkdale, Liverpool, then he was in Pentonville for two days before being sent to Millbank, London, where his job was to pick oakum. After nine months, he was moved to Dartmoor, Devon for a year. From January 1879 until his release in 1882 he was at Portland in Dorset, where he was put to work quarrying.

There are weekly records of marks and gratuities awarded to Frederick. Habitually, he earned 56 marks a week and 11d gratuity each month. By July 1880, this had increased to 7d a week and a running total of his earnings was kept. From May 1881 onwards, no gratuities were earned. Was Frederick no longer working, or was the £3 that he had accrued the maximum allowed? His only offence whilst in prison occurred during the first month of his sentence, when he was found to have 'a communication written in the fly leaf of a religious book and a leaf of *Leisure Hour* in his possession', for which he forfeited sixty remission marks.

The evidence suggests that his family were supportive whilst he was in prison. There is a list of Frederick's incoming and outgoing correspondence. It seems that he wrote to his wife approximately every six months; it is likely that this was all that was allowed. He also wrote to his recently married sister, Mrs Lizzie Patchett of Salford House, Blackburn. Once Frederick was at Dartmoor, the frequency of his letters increased to one every two months. Several different addresses are given for his wife, all in the north-west of England. He also occasionally wrote to another sister, Mrs W.J. Polding, whilst he was in Dartmoor. In June 1879, it is recorded that his wife visited him in Portland. There is a list of requests made by Frederick. These included, on January 1878, asking for permission to write a letter in place of a visit but this was not allowed. In February 1879, he was granted a visit from his wife, son and brother-in-law. He also asked that he might be issued with shoes, rather than boots, on discharge; this request is annotated 'if possible'.

Frederick's medical record stated that he had had 'brain and rheumatic fever' before being imprisoned but he was never in hospital whilst in gaol. His entry in the Habitual Criminals' Register in MEPO6, lists his distinguishing marks as being a scar under the right eye, moles on his right side, the back of the right thigh and on his neck.

Although Frederick married in the Anglican church and his son was baptised in the Church of England, he is recorded as being a Roman Catholic in his Penal Record in PCOM3. It is interesting that when his son was enrolled in Salesbury Church of England School, in 1882, he was marked as being exempt from religious instruction.

On 31 July 1882, Frederick was released on licence and was said to be intending to seek employment in Blackburn. It appears that the events that led to his imprisonment were an aberration and that Frederick settled into family life after he left prison. Three more children were born in the 1880s, one, a daughter Ethel, dying in infancy. In the 1891 census, the family can be found living at 109 Nashville Street, Salford; Frederick was working as a clerk. His eldest son was a boarder at Ampleforth Roman Catholic College. The Railtons moved to a four-roomed property, 11 Osbourne St, Farnworth, Bolton, Lancashire and another son, Joseph Leonard, was born in 1897. Osbourne Street was to be Frederick's home until his death in 1921. The 1911 census reveals that Frederick was a builder's clerk; his three children, then aged between 14 and 24 were working in the cotton mills. By 1921, shortly before his death, Frederick had retired. His youngest son, who was still living at home, was a miner and the family had a lodger. It seems that Frederick's criminal activities had led his children to have a less affluent upbringing than Frederick's own.

Chapter 3

IMMIGRATION AND ETHNICITY

This chapter contains quotations from documents that include terms regarding race that are now unacceptable.

Throughout the centuries, incomers to Britain have been ostracised or persecuted. Fear of difference has left certain ethnic groups on the margins. Within Britain, prejudice has been directed at specific nationalities and races at different times; often when those groups were perceived as posing a threat. For example, waves of anti-Semitism have occurred at intervals since the twelfth century; those from Ireland and the Caribbean have experienced ostracisation. Life was made difficult for anyone of Germanic origin during the world wars and at the outset of the recent COVID 19 pandemic, there were racist incidents directed at those with Chinese heritage. It is beyond the scope of this book to cover all those who might have experienced marginalisation as a result of their nationality or ethnicity, but some of the sources mentioned in this chapter will apply to many of those whose origins lay outside Britain.

The marginalisation of certain ethnicities was fuelled by the rise of the eugenics movement in the early twentieth century. Karl Pearson, leader of the Galton Library for National Eugenics advocated the creation of 'a homogeneous white race, whose fertility shall markedly dominate that of the black'. He also thought that other marginalised groups, including the disabled, criminals and the poor, should be prevented from having children.

Resentment of immigrants and calls to curb immigration are not new. This xenophobia resulted in attempts to document those who were deemed to be aliens. After the Reformation, many of those entering England from overseas would, at least initially, not be worshipping in the Church of England, therefore records of other faiths are relevant when searching for immigrants.

Poor relations with France in the fifteenth century led to a mistrust of foreigners. This resulted in increasing public pressure to limit the rights and movements of those from overseas, who were seen as a potential threat to social order. Anti-alien petitions were presented to Parliament. Restrictions were put on foreign merchants who were trading in England; they were obliged to register and subsidies were imposed. Assessment documents are available for most English counties in class E179 at The National Archives. More information about what survives can be found in the E179 database **www.nationalarchives.gov.uk/e179**; this database does not allow for personal name searches. In 1512, Henry VIII levied a poll tax that required aliens to pay at double the rate of natives. War with France in the 1540s resulted in restrictions being put in place, limiting immigration from France and requiring all those who were French born to take out denization.

Denizations were first granted in 1370s. To be granted denization, it was necessary to take an oath of allegiance to the sovereign and to pay a fee. The amount varied from £2 to £50, according to status. Denization gave those born abroad similar rights to those born in England. They were able to own property or land but were not able to inherit it. Although denization entitled an individual to have cases heard in English courts, it did not specifically confer the right to vote. Aliens paid higher rates of duty on exports and imports and denization did not reduce these taxes. The cost of denization was prohibitive for some, so the records are not a complete list of all incomers.

From the sixteenth century, further rights were conferred on those who became naturalised, but until 1844, this required a private Act of Parliament. Until 1949, any resident of the British Empire or the Republic of Ireland was automatically a British subject. From 1949 until 1981, Commonwealth residents could register as British citizens, without necessarily moving to the UK. All those born in Ireland after 1948, however, had to apply for naturalisation if they wanted British citizenship. From 1981, anyone from anywhere in the world went through the same naturalisation process. It is important to remember that many immigrants did not take out naturalisation or denization.

The Acts of Parliament leading to naturalisation can be seen at the Parliamentary Archives **www.parliament.uk/business/publications/parliamentary-archives**. It is possible to use a library subscription to search Parliamentary Papers **www.gale.com/intl/primary-sources/state-papers-online** but pre-1844 references to the private acts of Parliament may just give name and occupation. Original records of successful naturalisations, held by The National Archives in class HO334, include naturalisation

Emigrants Leave Ireland, *by Henry Doyle (1827–1892), from Mary Frances Cusack's Illustrated History of Ireland, 1868. Image in the public domain.*

certificates, with details of birthplace and date, parents, spouse, children, occupation, address and date of arrival. Those for 1870–1916 are available on Ancestry, which can be accessed via a link on the useful National Archives' research guide. Case Papers relating to naturalisations also include character references and, from 1878, police reports.

Naturalisations and Denizations for 1509–1800 have been indexed by the Huguenot Society, for all those involved, not just Huguenots.

These are available on the Internet Archive **https://archive.org**. For 1603–1800, there is an index at The National Archives. Transcriptions for 1609–1960 are available on The Genealogist subscription website **www.thegenealogist.co.uk**, to those with a diamond subscription. These reveal, for example, that Charles Secondat, who had been born in Bordeaux, France, was naturalised in October 1795. His residence was stated to be Soho Square, Westminster.

The England's Immigrants' Database **www.englandsimmigrants.com** contains the names of 64,000 foreigners residing in England between 1330 and 1550 and gives plenty of detail about the background to these sources. The database is compiled from Letters of Denization and Alien Subsidy records, which are held at The National Archives in classes E179 and C67. It includes information from subsidies raised specifically from first generation immigrants who arrived between 1440 and 1487 and from the lay subsidy of 1523. This taxed both aliens and the native born, but aliens were taxed at a higher rate. Assessment and collection of this subsidy was done on a county by county basis, so records vary. The England's Immigrants' Database contains details from these returns for a number of selected counties and towns, using the most complete surviving assessment for each place. These include Cornwall, Devon, Dorset, Somerset, Norfolk, Suffolk, Essex, Yorkshire, Lincolnshire, Rutland and the towns and cities of Canterbury, Winchester, Southampton, Bristol, Oxford, Reading and Coventry. Unfortunately, no returns survive for London.

Looking at the details of what is on the database for Devon for example, it is revealed that:

> A group of documents survives for the collection of the 1483 subsidy, including not only two detailed inquisitions containing the taxpayers' names, nationalities and places of residence, but also the particulars of account listing which people had actually paid and which had not. The largest single national grouping was the Flemings, followed by the French and a few Scots, but the people listed were a varied group, including a Portuguese tailor in Barnstaple, a man with the surname Goldsmith from Cologne, and, rather intriguingly, a Jacobus Black, living in Dartmouth and described as having been born in 'Indea' or 'Judea'. Given that the spellings would be indistinguishable, whether this refers to India or Judea (i.e. the area of modern-day Israel) is unclear. The alien population of the county was concentrated in the south coast ports and towns, most notably Exeter itself, Plymouth, Sidmouth, Topsham, Dartmouth and Totnes, although Barnstaple and Black Torrington in the north were also represented. No details of the 1487 tax are known.

From 1792, the registration of aliens was a function of the Quarter Sessions Courts, whose records are in county archives. The registrations show the name of the individual, their age, the length of time they had been in the country, where they were from, their address and occupation. The Aliens Act of 1836 required immigrants to provide their nationality, port of entry and occupation. These records are at The National Archives. Alien Arrivals, arranged by port, for 1810–1811 and 1826–1869, are available on Ancestry, as are Aliens' Entry Books for 1794–1921 and Home Office correspondence. Aliens' registration cards for 1918–1957 are in class MEPO35 at The National Archives. They are only available for those born more than 100 years ago and copies can be obtained from The National Archives' website. They give name, date of birth, date of arrival in the UK, marital status, children, address, employer's name and address, date of naturalisation and a photograph. They may be annotated with changes of address, employment or marital status.

The National Archives holds Inward Passenger Lists for those arriving in the UK from ports outside Europe and the Mediterranean between 1878 and 1960 in class BT26. These are available on Ancestry. Note that many would have arrived from a European port and are therefore not included.

Discrimination on the grounds of ethnicity is exemplified by the treatment of those of the Jewish faith. Moneylending did not sit well with the tenets of Christianity, so, in the eleventh century, William I invited Jewish financiers to come to England from Rouen and they continued to finance subsequent Norman kings. The financial acumen and prosperity of many of the Jews bred resentment and in 1190 and 1191, a series of anti-Semitic riots swept eastern England, from York to London. In 1255, the Jews of Lincoln were accused of murdering a young Christian boy. Despite a lack of evidence, eighteen were executed for this crime. The Jews were expelled from England in 1290 and had no right of residence or worship in the country for more than 350 years. Despite this, irrationally, the Jews were blamed for the Black Death of 1348; it was thought that they had caused the sickness by poisoning the drinking water. In Europe, this resulted in a widespread genocide, with thousands of Jews being put to death by burning.

In 1656, Oliver Cromwell invited the Jews to return and this led to the arrival of Ashkenazi Jews from Holland and Bohemia. Further waves of Jewish immigration were sparked by persecution. Those seeking refuge from the Iberian inquisition arrived in the seventeenth and eighteenth centuries. Between 1880 and 1914, Sephardic Jews from Russia settled in England and in the 1930s, the persecutions of the Nazi regime saw Jews arriving from Germany, Austria and Poland.

Those of Jewish origin can be difficult to identify in non-denominational records, as religion is rarely specified. The names of individuals may provide a clue, although surnames might be anglicised. Old Testament forenames were favoured by those of the Jewish faith but were also popular amongst Protestant non-conformists. Their faith required Jews to live within walking distance of a synagogue; so, anyone suspecting that their ancestors might have been Jewish, should search for a synagogue nearby. The 1851 ecclesiastical census, which is available online at **https://discovery.nationalarchives.gov.uk/details/r/C8993**, lists all places of worship at that date. For the nineteenth and twentieth centuries, The National Archives recommends searching for a synagogue in the *Gazette*, which is freely available at **www.thegazette.co.uk**. They also suggest searching for a Jewish school in the Discovery catalogue using the record class ED and the advanced search term 'Jewish'. Anyone interested in early Jewish immigration should look at The National Archives' guide, *Jewish People and Communities in Britain and its Former Colonies*, which gives suggestions regarding looking for Jewish people in financial records and in documents relating to their persecution. For the seventeenth and eighteenth centuries, The National Archives advocates consulting collections of petitions, orders, letters and grants created by government officials. State Papers can be accessed online via a library subscription.

Synagogue records include lists of birth, marriage and death and bar- and bat-mitzvahs. The Bevis Marks Hall in London **www.bevismarks.org.uk** has a collection of Jewish registers dating from 1687 to 1837. Its publications include birth registers 1780–1887 and circumcisions performed between 1715 and 1785, with many details of parents, grandparents and godparents. The 1734–1793 General Registry of Births

The Alien Invasion, *Immigrant Jews in the Transit Shed at Tilbury c.1891. Image in the public domain, accessed via Wikimedia Commons.*

'not baptised in the established church', which is at College of Arms **www.college-of-arms.gov.uk**, relates predominantly to Jews, Catholics and Moravians and may be useful.

The National Archives' guide *Nazi persecution and the Holocaust* gives advice for searching for victims. A freedom of information request may be required. The guide also gives details of relevant records that are held elsewhere.

Some of our ancestors might have been able to escape marginalisation by attempting to hide their ethnicity. For those who were Black, their ethnic heritage was incontrovertible and sadly, they were liable to be a victim of prejudice and discrimination. Our views on enslavement have changed; now the concept of enslavement is abhorrent. In the past, the enslavers were regarded as those who were making sound economic decisions. Some who were associated with the slave trade may also have been philanthropic with the ensuing wealth and were therefore celebrated as pillars of society. Many family trees contain individuals who profited from the enslavement of others of a different race. The fact remains that there were over 12,000 known slaving voyages that left from the UK and contributed to the enslavement of 3.5 million Africans.

It is clear that, during the past 500 years, many Black people can be found in Britain for reasons that are not related to enslavement. In fact, the concept of slavery does not extend to British soil, so, in law, any enslaved person who was brought to Britain was automatically free. In practice, this was not adhered to. Undoubtably, the presence of many Black people was a legacy of enslavement and evidence can be found in documents such as parish registers and in wills.

Despite the statement by Elizabeth I in 1596 that 'blackamoors have no understanding of Christ or his gospel' there are baptisms and burials in early parish registers that reveal that some individuals were Black. For example, we find the 1767 Liverpool baptism of 'Thomas Mr John Blundle's negro' and in Stradsett, Norfolk, the 1729 baptism of 'Elizabeth negro servant of Madam Buxton'. A slightly different slant on the issue is revealed in 1812 in Remenham, Berkshire, with an entry for the baptism of George Freeman that reads 'An African Negro boy brought by Captain Scobell from Sierra Leone, rescued by him from a Portuguese slave ship and supposed to be about 11 years old'. Sadly, George Freeman, alias Foray, 'boy servant to Rev. Scobell (rector), an African negro', was buried six years later.

Slave Registers for 1813–1834 are held at The National Archives in class T71, most of which are available on Ancestry. They can be searched by the name of the owner or the enslaved person, remembering that the names given for the enslaved might have been those imposed upon them by the enslaver.

Although the taking of new slaves was abolished in Britain in 1807, the Abolition of Slavery Act of 1833, freeing those who were already enslaved, did not come into effect until 1834.

The Legacy of British Slave-ownership website **www.ucl.ac.uk/lbs/** allows you to search for slave-owners in the British Caribbean at the time that slavery ended. The enslavers were compensated for the loss of the enslaved, but no reparations were awarded to those they had enslaved. The database includes biographical details of the slave owners, some of which include portraits.

The Legacy of British Slave-ownership database reveals that Reverend Robert Allwood, son of Robert Allwood, was responsible for the enslavement of 202 people. Born in Kingston, Jamaica in 1803, he was educated at Eton then Gonville and Caius College, Cambridge and was later a clergyman in Australia. In May 1835, he married Anna Rebecca, the daughter of Joseph Bush of Martinique. They sailed to Australia in July 1839 and he served as vicar of St James's, Church Street, Sydney from 1840 to 1884.

Here is an extract from the wealth of detail that the database gives about Peter Harris Abbott:

> Official assignee and pioneering accountant, of City of London, awarded with others the compensation for 25 enslaved people in Westmoreland. Born in St Kitts 1774 or 1775, the son of Peter Abbott and Jane Dijett [sic], recorded as a merchant at 121 New City Chambers Bishopsgate in London in 1812 and established as an accountant by 1823. Evolved from public accounting to specialisation in bankruptcy. He absconded to Brussels in 1841 and was himself declared bankrupt that year. At a meeting of his creditors at the Guildhall Coffee House, held 19/05/1841, his debts were totalled at about £17,500 with an additional falcations of £60,000 or £70,000. Assets listed included the furniture and plate in his house in Brunswick Square (£1200); 48 pictures, a heavily mortgaged property in Toxteth Park, Liverpool, some small insurance policies, and numerous shares. His house was to be auctioned on 15/06/1841 and was advertised as 'in complete repair, and contain[ing] an excellent dining-room, library, front and back drawing-rooms, communicating with large folding doors, eight good bed-rooms, china closet, entrance-hall, water-closets, large kitchen, butler's room, wine, beer and coal-cellars, and every convenience, with stabling for three horses, and coach-house in the Mews'.

A sale of his house contents was scheduled for the following day, including '1000 volumes of elegantly-bound books, 70 dozen of choice wines, and numerous fine paintings by artists including Rubens,

Caravaggio and da Vinci, Morland, and O'Connor'. The contents of his office at 10 Kings Arms Yard were also up for auction.

Peter Harris Abbott married Frances Maria Dyett in 1811 at St George the Martyr, Queen Square. Their daughter Ellen married Mark Dyer French, a barrister, in 1837, when her address was shown as Brunswick Square. Mark Dyer French was the son of the Virgin Island enslaver, also named Mark Dyer French.

Unexpectedly, there are also references to enslavement in the census returns. One such case is that of Emma. Emma appears in the 1851 census, living at 6 Middleton Road, Hackney. She is enumerated as 'Emma', with 'no surname' written underneath. Emma was 35, born in Africa and her occupation is listed as 'house servant, late a slave'. The householder was 65-year-old James Thornton 'retired from South America'. There is no clue as to what he had been doing in South America. Ten years later, Emma was still with the Thorntons at the same address. James's occupation remains obscure, 'retired from business'. This time, Emma was recorded as Emma Emancipated, as if emancipated were her surname and in the birthplace column the enumerator has written 'African free'. Her age was recorded as 50. James Thornton does not appear in the Slave Registers or in the Legacy of British Slave-ownership database. This raises questions about the status of Emma, as she appears to have been born after the 1807 Act. If she was born to an enslaved mother, why would she have been born in Africa?

It is a sad reflection that it is far easier to find information about the enslavers than it is about the enslaved.

It is not possible to write a chapter on ethnicity without mentioning DNA. Autosomal DNA test results come with ethnicity estimates. DNA is an emerging science and is continually being refined but these estimates are just that, an estimate. Each company generates suggested ethnicities using different data, which is why a person's profile may differ if they test with more than one company.

The same person tested with four leading DNA companies. Currently, their ethnicity estimates are as follows:

Company 1 – England and North-western Europe 62%, Wales 10%, Sweden and Denmark 9%, Germanic Europe 8%, Scotland 8%, Norway 3%.

Company 2 – Britain 39%, Scandinavia 23%, Ireland 21%, Central Europe 16%, Greece and the Balkans 2%.

Company 3 – Britain 95.6%, South Germanic 4.4%.

Company 4 – England 66.3%, Scandinavia 33.7%.

Had they tested at company 3 alone, they would not expect to look beyond Britain within the genealogical time frame. Testing only with company 2 would give them a very different perception of their ethnic background.

Not only do an individual's ethnicity estimates vary from company to company but the ethnic make-up suggested by a DNA test will be modified, as the base data that the company is using alters. With the current state of the science, ethnicities suggested by DNA results are, at best, possibilities and should not be taken as definitive proof of a particular heritage.

The Story of Catherine Eve

We first meet Catherine Eve in the pages of the baptism register for Corsham in Wiltshire. She was baptised in 1814, with no parents named, aged about 20, abode Jamaica and labelled as a mulatto, a woman of mixed race. It is not clear if Eve was her surname or a second given name. It always pays to turn the page in the register as the next entry, on the following page, is for Catherine's son George Edward, born to

People with baskets and sacks pick cotton on a plantation. *Coloured lithograph after J.R. Barfoot. The Wellcome Collection* **https://wellcomecollection.org/works/mf7r354u** *Used under Creative Commons CC-BY-4.0 licence.*

George Newman and Catherine Eve, 'mulatto slaves', and this implies that perhaps Eve was a surname.

Searching for other Newmans in the Corsham baptism register revealed an interesting entry for George senior who was baptised in 1808, with the note, 'a black brought from Jamaica by Mr Richard Newman, years of age about 20'.

It proved impossible to find out more about Catherine, her husband or son. There are no Catherines (with any surname) born in Jamaica in the 1851 census, so she had either died by then or perhaps returned to Jamaica. There are no obvious burials in the immediate area. Inevitably, she left her trail through that of her enslaver. The Legacy of British Slave-ownership database includes an entry for Richard Newman, who owned plantations in St Elizabeth and Manchester, Jamaica, where more than 200 enslaved people worked. Although Richard Newman's slaves are listed in the Slave Registers, the records are for the period after George Newman and Catherine Eve were in Wiltshire, so they do not appear.

Chapter 4

PROSTITUTION

Throughout history, women have sold their bodies for money, or in return for rewards in kind. For some, this was a conscious career choice but most took to the streets out of necessity, in order to feed themselves or their families. Prostitution was generally regarded as a threat to the moral well-being of the community, damaging to social order and a danger to the health of the nation. With a few exceptions, prostitutes found themselves on the margins of society. It is very difficult to estimate the extent of prostitution. Social reformer Henry Mayhew suggested that there were 80,000 prostitutes in Victorian London, but at best this was a guess; his figure may have been a significant overestimate.

The general attitude of condemnation was fuelled by the church's desire to control people's sexual behaviour. This led to attempts to regulate and prohibit soliciting and criminalise those who were paid for sexual favours. Social reformers organised campaigns that sought to rehabilitate individual prostitutes. This reached a height during the Victorian period, when a number of homes for fallen women were set up for this purpose. Usually, life skills, literacy and household tasks were taught, alongside religious and moral education. Charles Dickens was involved in the administration of one such home, Urania Cottage, an institution for the reformation of London prostitutes that aimed to fit them for emigration to Australia. Some institutions, such as the notorious Magdalene Reformatories, adopted severely punitive regimes. Many of the inmates were not prostitutes but women who had been unfortunate enough to have an illegitimate child at a time when society frowned upon sex outside marriage.

Occasionally, a full-time, professional prostitute might be taken as a mistress by one client. If he was well-off, this could open the doors to high society and a comfortable lifestyle with plenty of perks. Barbara Villiers' role as Charles II's mistress enabled her to procure positions on the Privy Council for her friends and she became the Countess of

Castlemaine. Alice Keppel, mistress of Edward VII, was a sought-after society hostess. Although the few who were mistresses of the king, or of others in high office, often wielded considerable social and political power, this was the exception. The vast majority of prostitutes were, and remained, working class and the situation was very different at this end of social scale. Those driven by poverty, often orphans, might take up the 'trade', or be forced to do so, at ages as young as 12. Young girls fetched higher prices, not just because of their youth but because they were less likely to be diseased.

In April 1841, the *Staffordshire Advertiser* contained the following report:

> William Parr and John Parr, father and son, George Buckley, John Machin, potters from Tunstall, Emma Hinds and Ann Birch, two girls of not more than 15 years of age, were brought up by Madden, the officer, who stated that he had found them making a great noise in a low brothel kept by the two girls, who had no parents. The men, who are all advanced in years, excepting Parr jnr., received a severe reprimand. The two children were ordered to be taken to the workhouse.

In their research, genealogists may come across women who had several illegitimate children. Take Letitia Gilbert of Great Bedwyn in Wiltshire for example. Letitia bore four illegitimate children, the first when she was 18 and the fourth at the age of 32. Three years later, she married and had a further four children. There is no suggestion that her husband was the father of all or any of the children who were born before the marriage. Further investigation into the Gilbert family shows that Letitia's sister, Elizabeth, also had four illegitimate children, over a period of nineteen years and that other sisters, Ann and Maria, had one illegitimate child apiece. Taken together with the fact that their cousin, Amy, also had three illegitimate children, it is starting to look as if this was a family business.

These ladies could, of course, each have been in a stable relationship with someone who was unavailable to marry, but in an era of inefficient or non-existent contraception, having an illegitimate child was an occupational hazard for those who engaged in prostitution. Finding a family member who gave birth to a succession of children outside wedlock should at least prompt questions about her lifestyle.

Women, particularly those who lacked a father or husband, often struggled to support themselves. They were hampered by low wages, uncertain employment prospects and domestic responsibilities that made undertaking paid work difficult. As a result, it was not unusual for women, including married women, to resort to boosting their income by selling their bodies. These occasional prostitutes were known as 'dolly-mops'. There are many other euphemisms and slang terms for a prostitute and these find their way into the records. Look out for such expressions as, 'fallen woman', 'a woman of easy virtue', 'a woman of bad character', 'a woman of the night', 'a woman of the town', or even 'a nymph of the pavé'. Other historical words for women who were regarded as promiscuous include, 'doxy', 'strumpet', 'harlot', 'wanton' and 'trollop' but these terms do not necessarily imply that money changed hands.

Although the 'great social evil', as prostitution was labelled in the nineteenth century, is mentioned in contemporary writings, such as newspapers, pamphlets and sermons, finding information about individual prostitutes is much more difficult. It would be very rare for a woman to refer to herself as a prostitute; this label would be attributed to her by those in authority, who were compiling the records. Occasionally, a baptism register might label a mother as a prostitute. The perpetual curate who served the Abbey Church of St Mary and St Sexburga, Sheppey in Kent in the 1820s, used the term on several occasions; perhaps he considered every mother of an illegitimate child to be a prostitute.

Sometimes prostitutes are revealed in the census returns, particularly if they are in institutions at the time. More frequently, they are disguised in the myriad domestic servants, launderesses and milliners. There are 446 individuals in the 1881 British census with the occupation 'prostitute'. The oldest was 63-year-old Catherine Buckley, a widow from Ireland, who, together with other prostitutes, was in prison in Usk in Pontypool. Many prostitutes can be found in the female lock-up hospital and asylum in Paddington. The youngest, Elizabeth Ross from Gravesend, was just 10 years old. This is unquestionably appalling, especially when viewed with a twenty-first century mindset. It is, however, important to set this against the context of the time and the fact that it was legal for a 12-year-old girl to marry, with parental consent, until as late as 1929. Of course, marriage at this age would have been almost unheard of by the second half of the nineteenth century, although marriages of 14- and 15-year-old girls can be found. At odds with the law governing marriageable age, was the raising of the age of consent from 12 to 13 in 1875 and to 16, ten years later.

Details of named prostitutes are most likely to be found in court records, or in newspaper reports of trials. For example, a defendant might be labelled as a prostitute in cases involving soliciting, brothel keeping, seeking or obtaining an abortion, attempting to conceal the birth of a child, or infanticide. Sexual excess was grounds for incarceration, so prostitutes might be found in asylum records.

A series of Contagious Diseases Acts were passed in the 1860s, following concerns at high levels of sexually transmitted infections amongst the armed forces. The prevalence of syphilis at this time is borne out by looking at service records. Initially, the police had the right to arrest women found near barracks and in ports but later the jurisdiction was extended. These women were subjected to compulsory examination and those infected were forcibly hospitalised in 'Lock Hospitals', or if these were full, workhouse infirmaries, for a period of between three months and a year. It is possible that workhouse admissions' registers may allude to the reason for their admission. Those who refused to be examined could be sentenced to imprisonment, often with hard labour. These acts also impacted on women who were not prostitutes but who were in the wrong place at the wrong time; it should not be assumed that all those held under the Contagious Diseases Acts were prostituting themselves. Not infrequently, married women who were entirely faithful became infected with venereal disease because of their husbands' behaviour. The impact on women who were not prostitutes was one reason why there were many protests against these acts. Another bone of contention was the fact that no checks were made on the male clients. Eventually, campaigns led by Josephine Butler and others involved in the fight for women's suffrage, led to the acts' repeal.

Although the women involved in prostitution were marginalised, their customers were not. A visit to a prostitute might be regarded as

Ladies National Association for the Repeal of the Contagious Diseases Acts, image in the public domain, accessed via Wikimedia Commons.

a badge of office, or a course of action that was taken by a considerate man who wished to spare his wife his attentions. The widely held opinion was that men's sexual appetites were greater than women's and that women derived no pleasure from intercourse. The Church stated that sexual relationships were purely for the purposes of procreation. Sex outside marriage was frowned upon and was punishable in the church courts. The general view was that sexual excitement was potentially harmful to a woman's physical and mental well-being. At the same time, sexual continence was regarded as damaging to men's health. Prostitutes were, therefore, seen as a necessary evil, providing an essential service for unmarried men and for husbands who were not engaging in regular marital relations with their wives.

Underlining the benign attitude towards men who used the services of prostitutes is the existence of published guides to the whereabouts of brothels. *Harris's List of Covent Garden Ladies* was an annual publication, produced from 1757 to 1795, that listed the woman's age, appearance and accomplishments, such as singing and dancing. In addition, the reader was informed of the 'specialities' of her trade, her address and the price, which ranged from 5 shillings to £5. In the 1830s and 1840s,

A Harlot's Progress, *Hogarth. Image used under Creative Commons in the public domain.*

a similar publication for those seeking a London prostitute was the *New Swell's Night Guide to the Bowers of Venus*, which identified brothels and places frequented by prostitutes.

An unusually sympathetic viewpoint appears in the *Norfolk Chronicle* of 7 January 1786, which reported:

> There are those who maintain that female prostitutes are necessary to good order, and they argue from the necessity that a few should be sacrificed for the good of the community at large. If there were not prostitutes and brothels, say they, no man's house would be sacred from the violation of lust and brutality.

The article goes on to claim that there were 50,000 prostitutes in London and that 5,000 died annually. It concludes:

> Prostitutes have very improperly been stiled [sic] women of pleasure; they are women of pain, of sorrow, of grief, of bitter and continual repentance, without a hope of obtaining pardon, cut off from society, they become desperate. Yet let it be remembered, that he whose example should be followed by Christians, has shewn that their sins are to be forgiven.

According to the *South Wales Daily News*, in February 1877, Richard Henry Row, landlord of the Shades Tavern, in the inappropriately named Salubrious Passage, Swansea, was charged with harbouring prostitutes in his establishment. The police reported observing seventy-five prostitutes visiting the tavern in one evening, each leaving ten minutes later in the company of a man, many of whom were foreign sailors. A study of historical newspapers also reveals the bizarre nature of some of the beliefs that were held about prostitution. A writer to the *Louth and North Lincolnshire Advertiser* in 1861 claimed that the steep rise in prostitution was a direct result of the work of the Early Closing Movement, who were campaigning to secure a half day off for shop workers.

It is a mistake to consider prostitution only in terms of female workers. Attitudes to female sexuality meant that heterosexual male prostitutes were rare but those prostituting themselves for homosexual purposes were not. Like their female counterparts, many male prostitutes were young. Not only did they attract censure but they were regarded as being doubly culpable, as homosexual relations, whether paid for or not, were illegal in Britain until 1967.

Suggestions that a woman was a prostitute might be uncovered in records that have a very different purpose. The transcript of a list

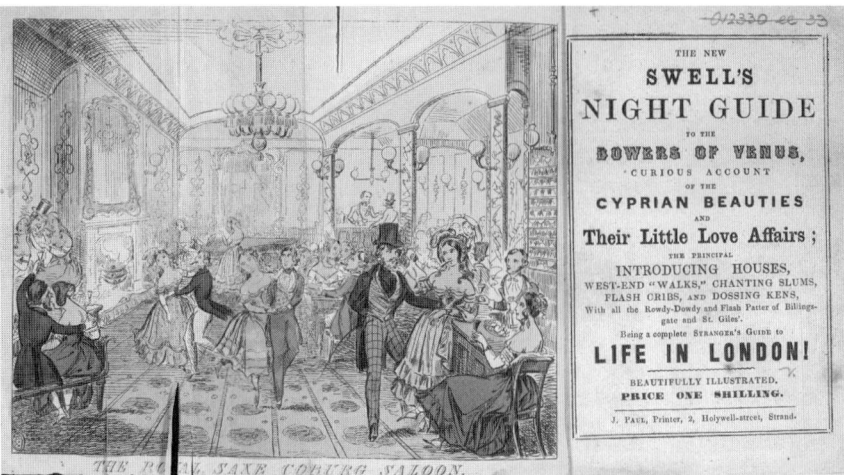

A Swell's Night Guide, c.1847. The British Library C.194.a.1217. Image in the public domain.

of Manchester victims of the 1832 cholera epidemic is available on Findmypast. The notes for 16-year-old Elizabeth Aspin read:

> Elizabeth Aspin, commonly called Crazy Bess, aged 16. Residence: Back Parliament-street. Employment: woman of the town [i.e. a prostitute]. Constitution: stoutish. Natural susceptibility: subject to diarrhoea after drinking. Predisposing cause: alternately starved and drunk, often sleeping in the street. Exciting cause: drunk on the Reform celebration day the day before her attack, cried passionately when Laurence [another victim] was taken to the hospital. Locality: crowding, filth &c. for the locality see case 181. Dates of attack and event: seized Friday, August 10th, at 11pm, recovered August 30th. Communication or non-communication: no known communication with Laurence nor anybody else.

Sadly, engaging in prostitution, might result in ill-health or premature death. Prostitutes ran high risks of contracting sexually transmitted diseases and this may be apparent on death certificates. 'General paralysis of the insane' as a cause of death denotes end-stage syphilis, although, of course, the majority of people who contracted syphilis were not prostitutes. In common with many other desperate women, prostitutes may have risked their lives when attempting to end an unwanted pregnancy. Methods might include herbal concoctions involving cuckoo pint, pennyroyal or parsley; hot baths and gin; or invasive surgical interventions, usually carried out by back-street abortionists in unsanitary conditions. In the absence of legalised abortion and efficient contraception, many prostitutes bore illegitimate children, another cause of marginalisation and this will be discussed in the following chapter.

The Story of Charity Platt

Charity Platt was the daughter of (William) Thomas and Susan Platt and was baptised in 1862 in Dalton-in-Furness, Lancashire, where her father was an iron miner. In 1881, she was working as a domestic servant for a baker in Preston. It was during the 1880s that matters began to go wrong for Charity. The newspapers and various court records paint a sorry picture. By the June of 1889, when she was sentenced to fourteen days with hard labour for being drunk and disorderly, Charity was living in China Lane, Lancaster. This street is described by Philip Martin on his History Geek website as follows:

> It was crammed with brothels, inns and lodging houses and with a touch of similarity between London's Whitechapel of the 1880s, although massively smaller. The area was overcrowded and with endless stories of crime. The working, living and sanitation conditions for those who lived in the area were horrendous. China Lane has always been labelled as a notorious neighbourhood, the centre of the poor.

Although this appears to have been Charity's first conviction, she was described as 'a woman of bad character', which is a term often used to describe a prostitute.

In January 1890, Charity was lodging with a man named Winder in China Lane. She was seen walking off with Winder's boots and when she was apprehended for this, she assaulted the police officer and was sentenced to two months with hard labour for robbery and assault. She was said to have been drunk at the time. By the end of 1890, her crimes had escalated and described as a 'woman of loose character', Charity appears to have been involved in a drunken brawl, during which John Coleman Nesbitt, with whom she was cohabiting, struck her across the mouth. Together, Nesbitt and Platt were charged with wounding John Smith with a knife. The case against Charity was dismissed.

In February 1891, Charity was involved in a knife attack on William Lockhart which took place in a lodging house in China Lane; it seems likely that Lockhart was a client. So, in the spring of 1891, the census records Charity as one of many prostitutes in Holloway Prison in London. The following week, banns were called in Lancaster for her marriage to none other than John Coleman Nesbitt. The marriage never took place and the banns register is annotated 'not married'. Was this because Charity was in prison? John Nesbitt, some five years Charity's junior, was living with his parents in 1891 and was perhaps persuaded to mend his ways and cease associating with Charity.

It did not take Charity long to find a new protector as, by the end of the year, she was married to Robert Lloyd. On 29 January 1893, their daughter Mary was born in Dalton. No birth or death records have been found for Mary but her date of birth is given in a school admissions' record. In July 1899, Charity was accused of assaulting her neighbour, Susannah O'Neil, but the case was dismissed. By 1901, she was living in Cable Street, Lancaster with her husband Robert, a general labourer and 8-year-old Mary.

In November 1901, Charity Lloyd, alias Platt, was sentenced to one month's hard labour for being drunk and disorderly in Lancaster. The description in the prison record, which is in class PCOM2 at The National Archives and available on Findmypast, reveals that she was 39 years old, 5ft tall, with an imperfect education and that her occupation was sewing. She had been born in Dalton and had four previous convictions.

Charity Lloyd, a machinist, paid a fine for being drunk and disorderly in August 1902. A month later, Margaret Thompson was charged with wounding Charity. Charity refused to press charges. By this time, Charity, who had recently come out of prison, had left her husband and was cohabiting with a man named Potter. School records show that Charity's daughter, Mary, had remained with her father, Robert, in Barrow but Robert and Mary have not been found after 1904.

In September 1906, having only come out of prison the previous week, Charity served another fourteen days in jail, with hard labour, this time for prostitution. She had two convictions for using obscene language in 1907. By the end of that year, she was convicted of receiving thirteen stolen chickens from Benjamin Clamp, knowing them to have been stolen. On hearing of her sentence to one month's hard labour, she said, 'Oh thank you I can do that on my head'. Charity's ongoing, toxic relationship with alcohol is unquestionable and in January 1908, she served another six months in prison for drunkenness.

Charity was charged with managing a brothel at 23 Worcester Street, Barrow, for the property's tenant, Benjamin Clamp, in February 1911. According to the press reports, the couple 'had lived together as man and wife for a number of years'. She was sentenced to three months with hard labour. This means that she was once again in prison for a census, this time being enumerated at Lancaster Castle. Charity claimed that she had been married for seventeen years and had one child, who was now dead but she may have lost contact with Mary and not known if her daughter was alive. Charity's occupation was listed as a sewing machinist.

On the 22 August 1911, Charity was yet again drunk and disorderly and in the same incident, her partner, Benjamin Clamp, was convicted of assaulting a police officer and 'living on Lloyd's earnings'. Just a month later there was yet another drunk and disorderly charge. This time, Charity had been found drinking rum in a barn with a Robert Johnson, probably a client. Charity claimed that she was about to visit her brother in Dalton, so perhaps she was still in contact with her siblings. In court she claimed, 'I couldn't have been drunk at 6 a.m.' Sadly, the evidence of her past life suggests otherwise.

The Calendar of Prisoners tried at the Assizes, found in class HO140 at The National Archives, with images available on Findmypast and Ancestry, provides a further description. She had a fair complexion, grey eyes and even at the age of 50, dark brown hair. She had a mole on her left cheek, both fourth fingers were deformed and her left thumb had been crushed.

In 1913, Charity was once again convicted of brothel keeping and was, by then, described as a launderess. Charity was sentenced to fifteen months with hard labour for inciting two men to commit robbery with violence. She caused a scene in court and attempted to attack the other two prisoners, James Holmes aged 21 and William Bowron aged 17. All three were convicted of assaulting and robbing William Crooks who was lying drunk in the street.

Unsurprisingly, the 1913 Habitual Criminals' Register and Police Gazette, which is available in class MEP06 at The National Archives, with images available on Findmypast and Ancestry, lists Charity Lloyd alias Platt. No further offences have been found after 1913. Did she become a reformed character, which seems unlikely given her past record, or perhaps she just got better at avoiding capture?

This is not quite the end of Charity's story. At the end of 1920, she married Alexander McLachlan, a Scottish seaman who was at least fourteen years her junior. In the 1921 census, the couple were living in one room at 122 Greengate, Salford. Alexander was out of work, having been previously employed as a marine fireman for the White Star Line. It may be that this was a short-lived relationship. By the time of the 1939 register, Charity had reverted to the name of Lloyd and was living at 2 Gavan Street in Blackpool, describing herself as a widow undertaking unpaid domestic duties. She died in Blackpool in 1952 at the age of 89.

Chapter 5

ILLEGITIMACY

Until relatively recently, there has been a stigma attached to births occurring out of wedlock, with children and parents facing social and in certain instances, legal, discrimination. This is reflected in some of the terms used to describe the children of unmarried women; pejorative language such as base-born, bastard child, misbegotten, or child of the people can be found in baptism registers and other documents. The precise definition of illegitimacy varies with time and place. In particular circumstances, the child of a married couple could be deemed to be illegitimate, for instance if the marriage was thought to be invalid, or if it could be shown that sexual relations between the mother and putative father had not taken place.

Both the mothers of illegitimate children and those who were themselves illegitimate, found themselves on the margins of society. In the nineteenth and early twentieth centuries, a woman giving birth to an illegitimate child might be incarcerated in an asylum on the grounds of 'moral insanity'. Punitive homes for 'fallen women' were established to house those whose were found to have had sexual relations outside marriage. An illegitimate child was regarded as being concrete evidence of guilt.

Statistics for the nineteenth century suggest that a quarter of all brides were pregnant and 7 per cent of children were born outside marriage, but there were marked regional differences. Prior to the advent of civil registration, in 1837, it is more difficult to estimate the extent of illegitimacy. Most researchers will encounter illegitimacy in their families; it usually becomes apparent when a baptism register or a birth certificate omits the father's name. Trying to identify the unnamed father can be problematic, although for more recent illegitimacies, DNA evidence might help in that regard. Sometimes the child's second forename will give a clue to the father's identity. Occasionally,

The Birth certificate of Albany Braund, from the private collection of Janet Few.

illegitimate children are named in their father's wills but that may only be helpful if the beneficiaries have been indexed.

It is rare that the circumstances surrounding the birth of a child whose parents were not married are known. More recently of course, it is not unusual for a child to be born of unmarried parents and this is often a lifestyle choice for the parents. In 2020, almost half of all births in Britain were to parents who were unmarried; many of these parents would have been in stable relationships. Until the later twentieth century, attitudes meant that deliberately deciding to have a child outside wedlock would be much less common. Perhaps the father was unwilling, or unable, to marry the mother. Possibly, the child was the result of rape or incest. Maybe the mother did not want to marry the father but societal pressures would make this less likely. In some cases, there may have been several potential fathers. There are instances when the parents marry shortly after the child's birth but the child would still be recorded as illegitimate, as they were born before that marriage.

My own grandfather's birth, in 1888, led to an interesting marginal note on his birth certificate. He was born a month before his parents married, but the birth was not registered until after the wedding. I have no idea why they did not marry sooner. I assume that, after the marriage, my great grandmother went alone to register the birth, but as her husband was not present and they had not been married when the baby was born, the registrar could not record a father's name on the birth certificate. My great grandfather had to attend at a later date, in order for the marginal note to be added, naming him as the father.

The child of a married woman was deemed to be the child of her husband, even if his absence would make this biologically impossible. Sometimes, a parish clerk or incumbent, having recorded the baptism with a husband and wife as the parents, made a terse comment. William Henry Driscoll was baptised in Stepney, Middlesex in 1830, the son of

Sarah Driscoll and Morris 'her lawful husband'. Next to the father's name, the entry is annotated, 'as she stated having been transported beyond the seas before she became pregnant of this child'. If the woman was married, the person making the entry in the register might go to particular pains to explain why the child was not that of the mother's husband. When John Palmer was baptised in Dedham, Essex in 1834, the son of Mary Ann Palmer, the register entry stated, 'John the husband of Mary Ann Palmer has been transported six years and the reputed father of the present child is Jonathan Cooke.'

Whether the mothers were married or not, reputed fathers were sometimes named in baptism registers, perhaps because of fears of incest in later generations but also because identifying the father might save the parish the expense of supporting the child. When Anne, the daughter of Anne Allen, was baptised in Brereton-cum-Smethwick, Cheshire, in 1680, Thomas Basson the younger was named as the reputed father.

An illegitimate child was the responsibility of the parish in which they were born. The unmarried mother and her child were likely to be a drain on the poor rates, so it was important to try to secure alternative financial support. Provision for the maintenance of illegitimate children and the chastisement of their parents, was set out in the Poor Law of 1576. Putative fathers were expected to provide for their illegitimate offspring. From 1733, Bastardy Legislation, as it was called, set out a system whereby efforts were made to identify the fathers, so that they could be charged for the maintenance of the child. This led to documentation and the resulting records are held in county archives. Unfortunately, survival is patchy and there are only a few online examples.

A bastardy examination of the mother required her to name names. Then a warrant might be drawn up, instructing the parish constable to apprehend the putative father. Affiliation orders or bonds would be signed by the father, undertaking to pay money for the mother's lying-in, followed by a weekly maintenance sum until the child was 14. Other options for the father would be to deny everything, which would be difficult in a small community – although he might help his case if he could cast aspersions on the girl's character. He could marry the woman or, if he was wealthy, pay her off, but if this was an option, it would normally have occurred before the authorities became involved. Alternatively, he could take the king's shilling and join the army. Particularly if the putative father was young, a bastardy bond might be signed on his behalf by a third party, promising to meet the payments if the father defaulted. Records relating to the maintenance of illegitimate children also include accounts of payments received.

A bastardy examination for Broadwindsor in Dorset reads,

> County of Dorset. The voluntary examination of Mary Roper of the parish of Broadwindsor in the said county single woman taken upon oath before me John James Golden Dowland (clerk) one of his Majesties Justices of the Peace in and for the said county this thirtieth day of July 1831. Who saith that she is now with child and that such child is likely to be born a Bastard and to be chargeable to the said parish and that Robert Purchase of the parish of Broadwindsor in the said county (yeoman) hath gotten her with child of the said child.

If parentage was disputed, the case might be heard in the Quarter Sessions Courts, whose records are in county archives. The ecclesiastical courts would often hear cases of a sexual nature; for this reason, they were sometimes called the bawdy courts. Those accused of fornication, adultery or bearing an illegitimate child, might be tried there. The surviving records will be found in diocesan record offices. These records can be difficult to use, as they are frequently unindexed and most are only available in local archives.

Both married and unmarried women, faced with an unwanted pregnancy, might attempt to procure an abortion; this was a particularly likely course of action if the child was to be born illegitimate. There was no legal way to terminate a pregnancy until well into the twentieth century. Any expectant mother who tried to do this herself, or anyone who helped a woman to bring on an abortion was committing a criminal offence. Under the terms of the 1861 Offences against the Person Act, the penalty could be life imprisonment. A test case in 1938 allowed abortion up until the twenty-eighth week of pregnancy, under very limited conditions, such as the rape of the mother, or if her life was in danger. It was not until 1967 that this was extended. There might be court records giving information about those accused of attempting to terminate a pregnancy, whether these attempts were successful or not, and newspapers might carry reports of the trials.

Sometimes, the mother of an illegitimate child would be desperate enough to murder her child, or an incident might occur that led to a charge of infanticide. If a case reached the Central Criminal Court (The Old Bailey) then the records will be at The National Archives, but in addition, information may be found on the Old Bailey Online website. For example, on 8 December 1680:

> Margaret Adams, of the Parish of St Brides, took her Tryal for Murthering her Male Bastard Child; the Evidence against her

was, that she being lately come to London, had got her a Service, her Mistress not perceiving that she was with Child, but lodged a little Girl with her, when she on the 28th of November last, was delivered without the knowledge of any, and rising early next morning went about her occasions, leaving the Child dead in the bed with her Mistresses Daughter, it being conjectured that she had smothered it with the Bed-cloaths, the which the Girl waking found, and called out, saying, there was a Child in the bed, whereupon several Neighbours coming in, found it to be so. Upon her Tryal she pleaded that the Child was still born, and that one John Ashmore, upon promise of Marriage so far prevailed as to deflour her, but upon the reading of the Statute in that case made and provided, she was found guilty of the Murther [*sic*].

A woman giving birth to an illegitimate child might take the desperate step of abandoning her baby. Not all foundlings were illegitimate but many would have been. The London Foundling Hospital was established by Thomas Coram in 1739 and children first entered two years later. Records relating to the hospital are at London Metropolitan Archives **www.cityoflondon.gov.uk/things-to-do/history-and-heritage/london-metropolitan-archives**.

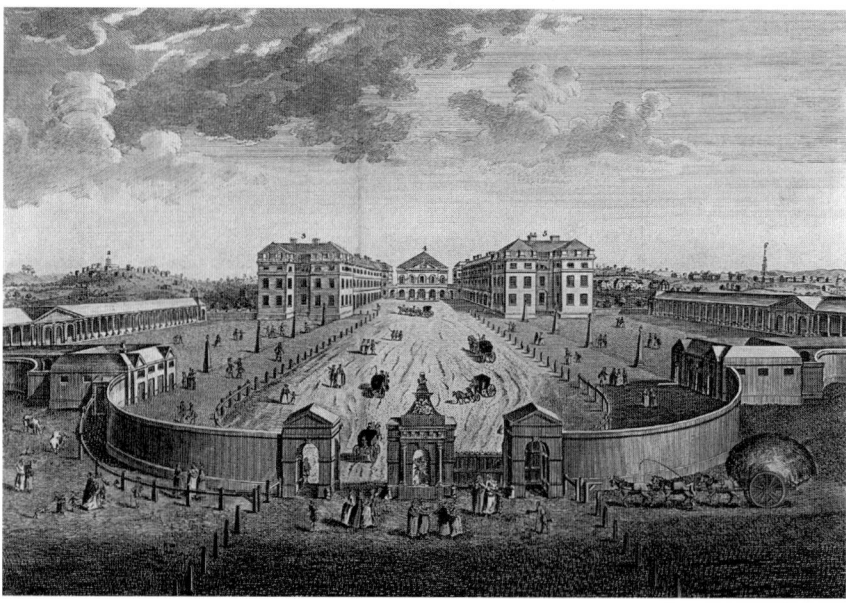

The Foundling Hospital, Holborn, London: A Bird's-Eye View of The Courtyard Numbered for A Key, *Coloured engraving after L.P. Boitard, 1753. The Wellcome Institute, library reference ICV13747, photo number V0013461* **https//catalogue.wellcomelibrary.org/record=b1194811**. *Used under Creative Commons.*

An unmarried woman who attempted to keep her child, would almost certainly have to put it in the care of someone else, so that she could earn a living. Baby farmers might take nurse children for a small sum of money. This could lead to the neglect of the children, as there was little profit for the foster parent if they spent lavishly on caring for the child. There was no legalised system of adoption in Britain until 1927, so these fostering arrangements were usually very informal.

In Scotland, the Kirk Sessions would investigate cases of 'antenuptial fornications'. The unmarried mother, or mothers of children who were born inconveniently swiftly after the wedding, would be examined and strongly encouraged to name the father. The father then had the opportunity to confess his sin, or attempt to deny responsibility. Both parents would be rebuked and might be expected to do penance at the door of the church for three Sundays in succession, in order to be accepted back into the congregation; they might also have to make a donation towards the relief of the poor.

Kirk Session records are held at National Records of Scotland and are available online at Scotland's People **www.scotlandspeople.gov.uk** on a pay-per-view basis. Indexes to Paternity Decrees for 1750–1922 and the Antenuptial Relationship Index for 1661–1780 are available on Findmypast. The Antenuptial Relationship Index reveals that Agnes Brown of South Leith named Gilbert Reid as the father of her child on 1 October 1668. Gilbert confessed and was rebuked.

Under the terms of the 1834 Poor Law Amendment Act, often called the New Poor Law, the responsibility for the upkeep of an illegitimate child was placed solely on the mother. There was no longer any legal mechanism for enforcing fathers to support their illegitimate children. If, however, the Board of Guardians became involved, because a father failed to pay maintenance for an illegitimate child, the authorities could take the father to court to recover the cost. Mothers of illegitimate children needing support under the terms of the 1834 act had to enter the workhouse, as there was no longer any out-relief for unmarried mothers. The system changed again in 1844, when mothers were able to apply to the Petty Sessions Courts for an affiliation order. Surviving records will be in county archives but many are no longer available.

Parishes, and later poor law unions, trying to reduce their outgoings on the upkeep of illegitimate and other pauper children, would seek ways of getting children permanently off their books. In the nineteenth century, the system of parish apprenticeship might be used. This is not to be confused with traditional apprenticeship, where children were taught a useful trade and masters agreed to provide a suitable standard of care and instruction. Parish apprentices, both boys and girls, might be as young as 3 and could be apprenticed for terms of up to twenty-one years to nebulously defined roles such as housewifery or husbandry. Householders were expected to take their allocation of parish apprentices and the system was open to the most appalling abuse.

Being illegitimate carried legal, as well as social, implications. As long ago as 1235, the Statute of Merton declared that 'He is a bastard that is born before the marriage of his parents.' This was significant as an illegitimate child had fewer rights, particularly when it came to inheritance. This discrimination continued until the twentieth century. The terms of the Legitimacy Act of 1926 declared that children whose parents subsequently married were legitimate; however, this was not allowed if either parent had been married to someone else at the time of the birth. In 1959, any child whose parents subsequently married was declared to be legitimate. The 1959 act applied to England and Wales only; the Legitimation Act extended this to Scotland in 1968. It was not until 1969 that the Family Law Reform Act allowed an illegitimate child to inherit if its parents died intestate.

The Story of Hannah Midgley
On the 1 June 1715, Hannah Midgley's son, William, was baptised in the West Yorkshire parish of Tong. No damning phrase was used to describe the infant but the word 'spinster' after Hannah's name tells its own story. It seems that Hannah was herself illegitimate, as Hannah, daughter of Esther Midgley of neighbouring Birstall was baptised in 1695. In the summer of 1714, Hannah had a relationship with John Ogden a local clothier. There is no way of knowing if this was a consensual relationship, or if John Ogden was Hannah's employer, or in some other position of authority that made it difficult for Hannah to refuse his advances.

The National Archives' Discovery catalogue reveals that West Yorkshire Archives hold a bastardy examination for Hannah and this document is browsable on Ancestry but does not come up in a personal name search. On 28 July 1715, justices George Tempest and Francis Lindley conducted Hannah's examination. Hannah said that, 'about thirteen weekes agoe she was delivered of a male Bastard childe within the said Township of Tong, which said childe already chargeable to the said towne and further saith that John Ogden late of Tong clothier is the sole father of the same and noe other person whatsoever.'

On the same day, Hannah Woodhead of Bradford swore an oath before the justices and 'saith that she practice the the Arte of a Middwife and was sent for to assisste Hannah Midgley in her extremity of childe bearing and that the said Hannah Midgley did declare in the extremity that John Ogden was the sole father of the said Bastard childe'.

Was Hannah Midgley in Bradford when she gave birth, or was the midwife summoned from the town some 5 miles away? Hannah would have been under considerable pressure to name the father of her unborn child, it might even be that the midwife's assistance would be withheld until she did so. What of John Ogden, said to be 'late of Tong'? Had he decided that it was in his best interests to move away, or was his departure unconnected with the pregnancy? In any case, he was required to pay 18 shillings for costs already incurred and a further 8d a week whilst young William was chargeable on the parish.

In 1719, Hannah Midgley married John Cook in Birstall. Apart from this, nothing further has been discovered about those in this story. After more than 300 years and with surnames that are not uncommon in the area, perhaps this is not surprising. It underlines the fact that those who are born out of wedlock do not always leave a significant trail in the records.

Chapter 6

THE INEBRIATE

For centuries, beer and ale were staple drinks for the British population, even children would drink small beer, which had very little alcoholic content. Labourers might expect an allowance of beer or cider as part of their pay; drinking alcohol was the norm. Alcohol consumption began to decline from the end of the seventeenth century. This is because alternatives, such as tea, coffee and chocolate became popular to quench thirst, rather than just as beverages for the rich to consume as part of a social ritual. This downward trend reversed during the first half of the eighteenth century, in part due to the government placing restrictions on the importation of brandy and the corresponding support for gin. It is estimated that the population was drinking six times more gin than beer at this time – hardly surprising as gin was much cheaper. During the 'gin craze' of 1730–1760, there were over 7,000 gin shops in London alone. The Gin Act of 1736, which significantly increased the tax on gin, led to riots. This forced the government to gradually reduce the amount of duty and remove it entirely in 1742. The Gin Act of 1751 saw a renewed attempt to limit the consumption of gin by restricting its sale to licensed premises.

Drunkenness was feared and condemned because it was seen as a threat to social order. Alcohol was regarded as contributing to moral degeneracy; inebriates were therefore on the margins of society. By the end of the eighteenth century, however, medical practitioners on both sides of the Atlantic were beginning to equate excessive alcohol consumption with illness. A notable publication was Benjamin Rush's *An Inquiry Into The Effects Of Ardent Spirits Upon The Human Body And Mind: with an account of the means of preventing, and of the remedies for curing them*, written in 1811. This and other studies, suggested that the alcoholic could be seen as being diseased, rather than depraved, but this outlook was very slow to take hold.

Gin Lane, *William Hogarth. Image in the public domain, accessed via Wikimedia Commons.*

The inebriates were not only ostracised because of their behaviour; their condition made it more likely that they would break the law, either to fund their addiction, or as a result of their conduct when drunk. Poverty often went hand in hand with drunkenness, partly because of the cost of alcohol but mainly because the inebriate would find it more difficult to gain employment. Excessive alcohol consumption also had an impact on their physical health, damaging the liver, lungs and brain and increasing the risk of heart attack or stroke. This meant that the inebriates were also likely to be criminalised, sick, or poor, or all three, marginalising them still further.

The Alehouse Act of 1828 required each town to hold an annual licensing meeting to grant licences to all premises selling excisable

Noah's Inebriation, *Giovanni Andrea de Ferrari 1630s. Image in the public domain, accessed via Wikimedia Commons, used under Creative Commons CC0 1.0.*

alcoholic beverages to be drunk on the premises. Victuallers' Licences were issued by the Quarter Sessions Courts and the records will be in county archives. A database of Warwickshire licensed victuallers is available online **https://heritage.warwickshire.gov.uk/catalogues-databases/licensed-victuallers-database**.

In an effort to encourage the drinking of beer, rather than spirits, notably gin, the Beerhouses Act of 1830 set a price of 2 guineas a year for a licence to brew and sell beer. Anyone who paid rates within the town could apply for a licence. As a result, thousands of beer houses were opened, in particular in the rapidly expanding towns of the industrial areas in the north and Midlands. It was hoped that increased competition would lower prices. To keep the costs down, beer for the poorer customers might be adulterated with poisonous substitutes for hops, including the plants Indian berry, also known as fishberry and *nux vomica*, whose seeds are a source of strychnine.

In 1870, the Bath MP, Dr Dalrymple, put a bill before parliament that allowed for the forcible institutionalisation of the inebriates, with the aim of removing them from the temptation of drink and reforming their lives. Although the bill was not passed, it did prompt the formation of a select committee on habitual drunkenness. In the 1870s, the cause of increasing instances of drunkenness was attributed to lenient punishments and individuals having additional leisure time as working hours reduced.

An Act of 1879 defined an habitual drunkard as someone who 'cannot be certified as a lunatic but who due to habitual intemperate drinking is dangerous to himself or herself or incapable of managing their affairs'. The term 'inebriate' also encompassed those who used drugs that had been ingested by drinking. Inebriates could pay for treatment at an institution run by the local authority, but places were limited and many alcoholics were excluded as they were unable to meet the cost.

The situation began to improve after the Inebriates Act of 1898 made provision for patients to be treated for up to three years in an Inebriates' Home. These homes were set up by the local authorities with the aid of government funding. Anyone who had four criminal convictions for drunkenness, or for crimes where drink was a factor, was eligible. The homes were certified by the government, but the authorities were slow to establish these institutions and provision remained inadequate.

By the end of the nineteenth century, there was an increasing awareness of the impact of drunkenness on physical health. A survey conducted by the Medical Officer of Health for Liverpool, in 1899, highlighted high rates of stillbirth and infant mortality in the children of mothers who drank excessively. Another enquiry found that the children of alcoholic mothers were twice as likely as children of sober mothers, to die before their second birthday.

The *Preston Herald* of 2 November 1901 commented on the second annual report of the Lancashire Inebriates Board, stating that the five Lancashire inebriate reformatories established under the act of 1898–9, had 416 beds available and that 16 males and 128 females had been admitted in the previous year, 4 of the women being under 21. 'Some committals proved to be certified lunatics, and over 25 per cent of the committals were mentally deficient, so long as they were drinking. Their eccentricity and violence was ascribed to their habits.'

Although certified homes were inspected, there were uncertified homes, run by private charities, where conditions were unsatisfactory. In 1907, the *Leominster News and North West Herefordshire & Radnorshire Advertiser* reported the escape of five women from the Southern Counties Inebriates' Reformatory. The women appeared in court at Lewes, Sussex and cited a catalogue of grievances, describing the home as 'a dirty, filthy place', unfit for human habitation. The women were each sentenced to two weeks in prison, with hard labour, for absconding.

Nineteenth-century licensing laws limited the hours during which alcohol could be sold; with the Sunday Closing Act of 1881 prohibiting all alcohol sales in Wales on a Sunday. Under the terms of the Sale of Liquor to Habitual Drunkards Licensing Act of 1902, lists of those with a history of convictions for drunkenness were kept by the local authorities. These were circulated to licensed premises who were instructed not to serve those who appeared in the books. The books include photographs of the habitual drunkards, along with their name, aliases, age, abode, occupation, a physical description and details of their most recent conviction. The book for Birmingham is on Findmypast and Ancestry.

The 1902 act allowed for an inebriate wife to spend time in a reformatory, as an alternative to being granted a separation order. Other acts, such as the 1904 Prevention of Cruelty to Children Act, meant that women could be detained if their drunkenness led to them neglecting their children. One such was Mabel Brooks, of Lewisham, Surrey, who was sent to the Southern Counties Inebriates' Reformatory in 1903 after her child was killed by rats whilst she was out drinking.

Concerns about the impact of alcohol consumption on the war effort meant that a section of the Defence of the Realm Act of 1914 curtailed the opening hours of public houses to a few hours at lunchtime and evening opening that began at 5.30 or 6.30 p.m. and ended at 10.30 p.m. The tax on alcohol was also increased. These regulations were not significantly relaxed until the 1970s in Scotland and 1980s in England and Wales.

Although there had been concerns about alcohol consumption in the eighteenth century, it was not until the 1820s that the Temperance Movement gained momentum. The first national Temperance Society was founded in 1828. In Scotland, John Dunlop founded The Glasgow and West of Scotland Temperance Society in 1829. At the same time, the Irish campaign was being spearheaded by Dr Edgar. Although the Chartists' principal objective was a call for universal suffrage, this working-class movement of the 1830s and 1840s also advocated for temperance.

Joseph Livesey was one of a group known as 'The Seven Men of Preston', who pledged to abstain from any alcohol in 1832. The term 'signing the pledge' was adopted for those who followed suit. Ann Carlisle was instrumental in setting up a temperance group for children. Two hundred children signed the pledge at the inaugural meeting in Leeds in 1847. This and other similar groups for children became known as the Band of Hope. The Band of Hope Union, to oversee the running of these groups, was created in 1855. By the end of the nineteenth century, there were well over 3 million members.

Initially, temperance involved abstaining from spirits but adherents continued to drink wine and beer. It quickly became more radical and there were many advocates of teetotalism. In 1853, the United Kingdom Alliance took a prohibitionist stance, campaigning to prohibit the sale of alcohol entirely. The Church of England Temperance Society was founded in 1862; there are records at Lambeth Palace Library **www.lambethpalacelibrary.org**. It was, however, the non-conformists, Methodists in particular, who were particularly strong advocates of temperance.

The British Women's Temperance Association was founded in Newcastle in 1876. Joseph Rowntree, founder of The Temperance Society, wanted England to adopt the Swedish principle of government control of liquor sales. Later, as part of the wartime measures, some public houses were nationalised. For example, in 1916, the government took over 363 pubs and 5 breweries in Carlisle, Cumberland. These establishments were not returned to private ownership until 1971. Until the end of the nineteenth century, alcohol was a much-needed source of calories for the working population. A drawback of the temperance campaigns was that those who signed the pledge might suffer from malnutrition as a consequence.

Although the term alcoholism is rarely found on death certificates before the late nineteenth century, there may be indications that alcohol played a part in the lives and deaths of our family members. Drunkenness frequently led to crime, so references might be found in the

Wine is a Mocker, *Jane Steen* c.1663. *Image in the public domain, accessed via Wikimedia Commons.*

court records, or in newspaper accounts. It is worth investigating local archives to see what they hold. What follows is just a small selection of might be discovered:

- Dundee City Archives has a list of inebriates in the city for 1903.
- Bristol Archives holds the records of the Stoke Hospital Group, which include the admissions' registers for National Institutions for Inebriates for many parts of England. These date from 1907–1936.
- The Lost Hospitals of London website has a list of London homes for the inebriate **https://ezitis.myzen.co.uk/briefhistoryinebriates.html**.
- There is a register of London patients at the Langho Inebriate Reformatory, established by the Lancashire Inebriates Act Board, for 1910–1914, at London Metropolitan Archives.
- The register of patients at Farmfield Reformatory for Female Inebriates 1900–1908, is also at London Metropolitan Archives.
- The Metropolitan Police's Habitual Drunkards List is in class MEPO 6/77 at The National Archives and can be browsed at Findmypast.
- There is an index to the names and ages of the children who signed the Band of Hope Register in Edinburgh between 1886 and 1908 on Findmypast.

The Story of Sarah Grosvenor
The first forty years of Sarah's life are obscure; she was born in the 1840s but even her birth surname is uncertain. Her birthplace was Dudley in the West Midlands, an iron mining and nail-producing area, just a few miles from Birmingham. The earliest confirmed sighting of Sarah is her appearance in the West Midlands Prisoner Photo Book. The original records are held in the West Midlands Police Museum **https://museum.west-midlands.police.uk** and the images are available on Ancestry. Accompanied by a photograph, Sarah Jones alias Grosvenor is listed with the admission date of 20 July 1885. Unfortunately, Sarah's entry is less informative than others, her age, height and hair colour have not been recorded. Her crime is 'not reporting'. It is unclear what this means; perhaps she was obliged to report to the police station but had failed to do so. No evidence of the crime leading to her appearance in this book has yet been found in the criminal records or newspapers; Sarah Jones is not the easiest name to search.

Once Sarah began to use the name Grosvenor, however, an extensive series of newspaper reports can be found. These catalogue her toxic relationship with alcohol and her frequent encounters with the courts. In December 1885, Sarah was sentenced to one month in gaol, with hard labour, for wilfully smashing a plate glass window, valued at £4, at the Bull's Head, in Smallbrook Street, Birmingham. In February 1888, Sarah

Grosvenor from Dudley was arrested for being drunk and disorderly, on a Saturday night, in George Street West, Birmingham, having been found singing and trying to dance. She refused to walk to the police station so an ambulance was sent for to transport her there. Sarah claimed that she was an invalid and that 'very little drink overcame her'. This was the fifth time that she had been taken into custody on release from prison. The magistrates showed leniency in the hope she might reform, as prison had not been effective and she was discharged. Clearly, the magistrates' forbearance was misplaced, as Sarah's convictions for drunkenness escalated.

Her court appearance in April 1889, was her forty-fourth and the magistrate commented that she 'was scarcely out of gaol two days together'. This time, her sentence was one month in gaol with hard labour. Within the next month, Sarah came before the magistrates a further six times. It seems that, on release from prison, Sarah would wander from inn to inn, in the hope that someone would supply her with drink. Her fiftieth appearance in court led the magistrate to describe her as a 'veteran drunkard'. On this occasion, she was in the Winson Green area and 'had a crowd of young men round her and was behaving most disgustingly'.

Sarah often took revenge on pub landlords who refused to serve her and one of these occasions reveals that she spent time away from the West Midlands. In January 1890, Sarah Grosvenor, launderess, of no fixed abode, was sentenced to fourteen days in prison in London, for wilfully breaking a plate glass window at home of Mr W.H. Dearling, the landlord of the Durel Arms, in Fulham Road. The Calendar of Prisoners, which is at The National Archives and available on Ancestry and Findmypast, refers to an appearance at Lambeth, Surrey Police Court at the end of January 1890, for malicious damage to two panes of glass, the property of Sarah Bennett. This gives Sarah Grosvenor's age as 43 and refers to eleven summary convictions for drunkenness, which is a significant under-representation. No reference to damage to the property of Sarah Bennett can be found in the newspapers. The sentence for this damage was a year in Millbank Prison, which suggests that this was a separate offence from the damage at the Durel Arms.

Although Sarah would have been released from Millbank before the 1891 census, she can be found in prison when the census was taken, this time in Holloway. Her occupation was listed as hawker and her birthplace given as Dudley, which accords with other records and makes it clear that this is the same Sarah Grosvenor. A drunk and disorderly charge for a Sarah Grosvenor back in Birmingham in June 1890, seems to refer to a different Sarah; as Sarah from Dudley was in Millbank Prison at this time.

Sarah again made an appearance in the Calendar of Prisoners in April 1892, when reference was made to the eleven charges of drunkenness and the 1890 conviction. This time, Sarah Grovier aka Grosvenor, aged 44, a launderess, was sentenced to twelve months in Holloway Prison for the malicious damage of property belonging to Charles Anderson.

By 1894, Sarah was once again in the Birmingham area. Her fifty-third appearance in court resulted in her spending a month in prison for wilfully breaking a window at The Royal Oak where she had asked for beer but as she had no money, she was refused. Unsurprisingly, Sarah was once again in prison in the 1901 census, this time at the lock-up in Steelhouse Lane, Birmingham.

The offending continued and by January 1903, Sarah had been accused in a Birmingham court 136 times with an additional 80 appearances before the magistrates in Liverpool. The Liverpool offences have not yet been found in the newspapers or court records, it is possible they were under the name of Jones, or another surname. Sarah was put on a blacklist of habitual drunkards 'under the terms of the new act'. Another fourteen days in gaol with hard labour followed in October 1904, when Sarah stole a glass of whisky worth 3d from the Royal Albert. The following year, Sarah, described as a 'neatly dressed elderly woman' made her one hundred and forty-eighth court appearance having been found drunk in Digbeth.

A report in the *Leominster News and North West Herefordshire & Radnorshire Advertiser* of 25 January 1907 claimed that the police described Sarah as 'one of the cleanest, best behaved and most useful women they have had to deal with'. It also reported that Sarah had now established a record amongst Birmingham's blacklisters, as she had over 200 convictions. She had spent time in an inebriates' home to no avail. Now in her sixties, Sarah was taken into the workhouse for seven months, before yet another drunkenness charge in June 1908. Her court appearance in August 1910, was the first for thirteen months and therefore the magistrate adjourned the case. Perhaps she had once again been in the workhouse and therefore had had no access to alcohol.

The 1911 census found Sarah, a launderess, boarding with Samuel and Florence Wilson and their four young children, in a four-roomed house at 2 Willes Road, in the Winson Green area of Birmingham. This time, her birthplace was given as Netherton, which is a small village on the outskirts of Dudley. Interestingly, the columns for years married and number of children have been filled in for Sarah and then crossed out. These suggest that she had been married forty-six years earlier and had had no children. No marriage has been positively identified. Ten years later, Sarah was a patient in the Western Road workhouse. Although her occupation was described as launderess, the details of her employer or former employer read 'mentally unable to give information'. Sarah died in 1923 and was buried in Witton Cemetery in Birmingham.

More information about Sarah's early life might help to explain her persistent offending. She is not wholly consistent about her age but it seems that she was born between 1842 and 1848 in Dudley, probably in the hamlet of Netherton. It has not been possible to conclusively identify a birth or pre-1891 census entry for Sarah as Grosvenor, Grovier or Jones and of course, her birth surname may have been something else entirely. There are no Sarahs, with any surname, of the right age in Netherton in the 1851 census; extending the search to Dudley gives too many possibilities.

Chapter 7

SICKNESS AND DISABILITY

Please note that this chapter contains historical terms for the disabled that are now unacceptable.

It was not just their physical condition that led to the sick and disabled becoming marginalised. Ill-health and disability often had a serious impact on an individual's ability to earn a living; working opportunities might be limited or non-existent, plunging them into poverty. Caring for a sick or disabled relative would be a responsibility that families were expected to undertake and, in many cases, this might have been a significant financial and emotional burden.

In order to better understand the way in which the sick and disabled were regarded and treated in the past, it is important to be aware of the beliefs surrounding medicine and the causes of disease. The theory of the four humours, first put forward by Hippocrates in the fourth century BCE and developed by Galen in the second century, persisted, to some degree, until the nineteenth century. This was based on the concept of balance. For good health, the four humours, blood, phlegm, yellow bile and black bile, had to be maintained in equilibrium. An excess of one humour resulted in sickness; therefore, medical, surgical and herbal 'cures' consisted of attempts to rebalance the humours. This explains the popularity of blood-letting and purging. Although an excess of phlegm might be treated with fennel, the surgical option was trepanation – drilling a hole in the patient's skull. The links between religion and sickness were strong and trepanning was also thought to release the evil spirits that were making the patient ill. Keeping the humours in balance was a preventative as well as a cure and those who could afford it would have blood let on a regular basis for this reason.

Despite the upsurge in scientific thinking during the Renaissance period, the concept of the four humours endured. This was largely because it was supported by the church. Putting forward ideas that challenged the theory was regarded as heresy and therefore potentially punishable by death. Notoriously, thirteenth-century philosopher and friar, Roger Bacon, was imprisoned for questioning Galen's ideas.

An imbalance of the humours was not the only perceived cause of ill-health. Beliefs in the influence of the position of the planets and astrology, were strong; a misalignment of the planets or an unfavourable conjunction of the stars was thought to result in sickness. Until the eighteenth century, an important part of medical diagnosis was casting the patient's horoscope. Certain signs of the zodiac were associated with particular body parts and this would indicate where the incision should be made for the letting of blood.

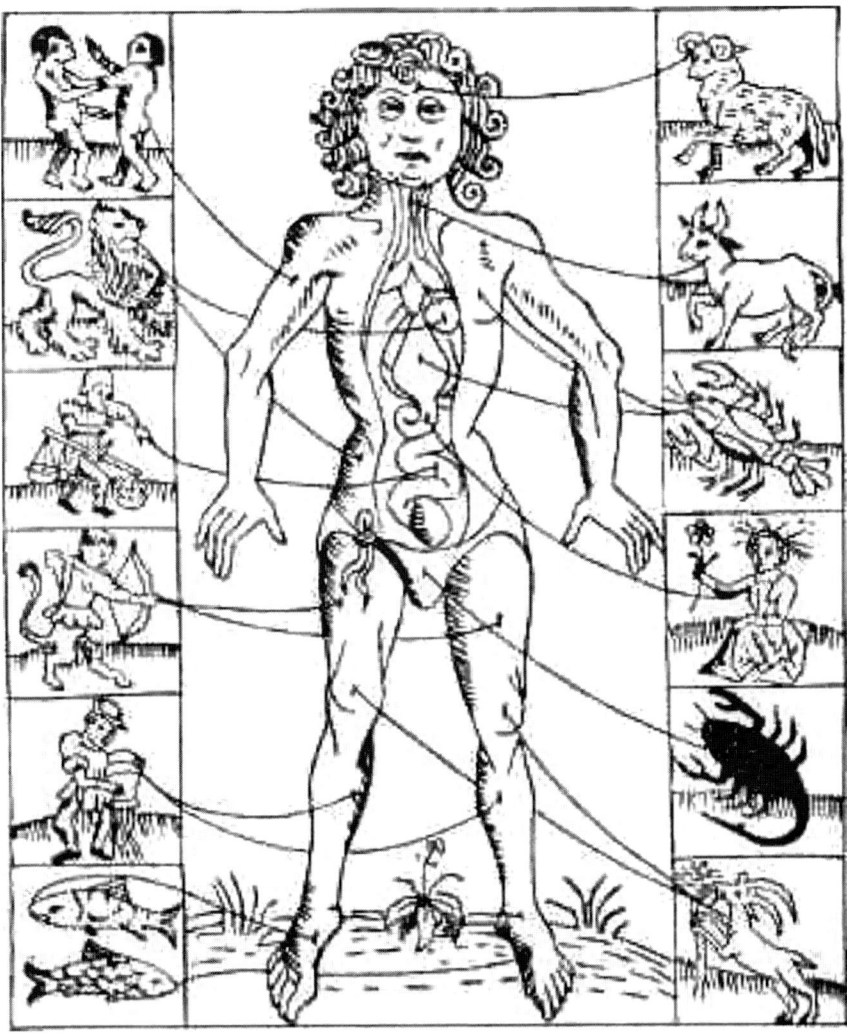

Zodiac Man 1702. *Image in the public domain, accessed via Wikimedia Commons.*

The belief that sickness might be a result of evil spirits or bewitchment, led our ancestors to attempt to prevent disease in ways that are now viewed as superstitious. Charms that were thought to be effective included stones with holes in and bezoar stones, which were mineralised balls of undigested material found in the stomach of animals, notably goats. Alternatively, ill-health might be regarded as a punishment from God, who, therefore, needed to be appeased. During the plague, flagellants were employed to beat themselves, in the hope of persuading God to remove the punishment of the epidemic.

Another theory, in popular use until the eighteenth century, was the Doctrine of Signatures. Most medicine was herbal and it was thought that God provided clues as to how a herb might be used, through its appearance. For example, the leaves of the *Pulmonaria*, also known as Lungwort, were though to resemble a diseased lung, therefore would be used for chest complaints.

The lack of understanding about the causes of disease made successful prevention or treatment difficult. The miasmic theory suggested that sickness was spread by bad air and this was often cited at times of epidemic. Although the concept of 'seeds of disease' was being discussed in the early nineteenth century, it was Pasteur's work in the 1860s that brought Germ Theory to public attention.

It is important to stress the impact of epidemics on our ancestors, who were faced with infectious diseases that were poorly understood and

Lungwort © *Janet Few.*

had no effective preventative or cures; this would have been a constant concern. The advent of inoculation and later vaccination began to reduce the instances of certain diseases. Lady Mary Wortley Montagu observed inoculations when visiting Turkey on her grand tour, in 1718, and she popularised the procedure in England. Inoculation involves giving the patient a mild dose of a disease, in order to render them immune to that same disease in future. Providing inoculations became profitable for those administering them, but it was an inexact process and could prove fatal if the dose given was too large.

It is Edward Jenner whose name is associated with the creation of the smallpox vaccine, paving the way for vaccinations for other diseases. In fact, Jenner was not the only person working on this process. With vaccination, immunity is created by giving the patient a milder but similar, illness, rather than the disease itself. Jenner noted that dairymaids rarely caught smallpox. This was because they often suffered from cowpox, which was less serious; therefore, vaccination with cowpox prevented the patient from contracting smallpox. Jenner was unable to explain his discoveries adequately and his ideas were greeted with ridicule. The government finally provided funding, and from 1853 smallpox vaccination was compulsory, leading to the eventual eradication of the disease. The vaccinations were often administered by the workhouse infirmary, so surviving smallpox vaccination registers may be with the workhouse records in county archives. For example, York Archives hold some for York Poor Law Union.

Alongside campaigns to encourage vaccination, there were many protests. In the case of smallpox, one of the more ludicrous suggestions was that having the vaccination might turn people into cows. Misinformation about vaccination abounded. According to a gentleman writing to the *Dundee Courier* in 1913, compulsory smallpox vaccination was responsible for both the Suffragette Movement and trade unionism. He wrote, 'the monstrosity called Militant Suffragette is the culmination of 50 years pollution of the blood of the nation among

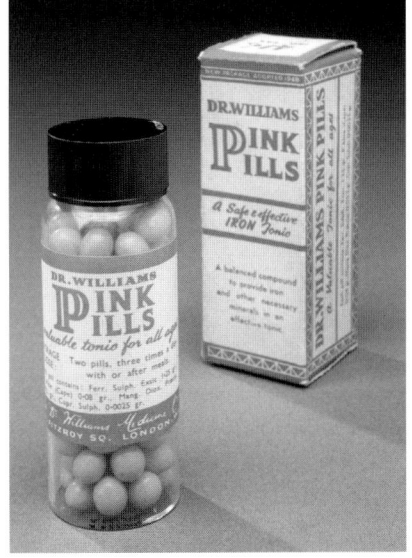

Dr Williams' Little Pink Pills, 1850–1920 Wellcome Images L0058211, Science Museum, London used under Creative Commons CC-BY-4.0.

women, while the senseless strikes led by blackguard demagogues shows insanity among men.'

Surgery was something to be feared and avoided if possible, but injuries, battle wounds and other complaints might necessitate a visit to the barber surgeon, whose role as a barber extended to medical procedures. Apart from blood-letting and trepanation, he was able to perform operations such as removing cataracts, extracting teeth and amputating limbs, with varying degrees of success. The descriptions of Samuel Pepys' seventeenth-century lithotomy (the removal of bladder stones), carried out in his neighbour's house, are renowned **https://earlymodernmedicine.com/surgical-spectators**. Fanny Burney wrote a description of her mastectomy, which was conducted in 1811 without the aid of anaesthetic **http://newjacksonianblog.blogspot.co.uk/2010/12/breast-cancer-in-1811-fanny-burneys.html**.

In many ways, surgical techniques that were being employed in the early nineteenth century had remained largely unchanged for 600 years. Treatment was very rough and ready and often carried out by poorly trained barber surgeons acting in haste. Three major problems accompanied surgical procedures; these were blood loss, pain and infection. Efficient anaesthetics were not available, meaning that patients died of shock due to the pain. Opiates were obtainable but their use was restricted by disapproval from the church, on the premise that pain was God-given and good for the soul. This meant that, during operations,

Barber Surgeon's Tools © Janet Few.

fully conscious patients had to be restrained by several burly assistants. Humphrey Davy began to use nitrous oxide (laughing gas) in 1800 but ensuring the correct dosage was problematic. Ether was successfully used in the mid-nineteenth century and Queen Victoria made the use of chloroform in childbirth respectable, by having it administered for the birth of Prince Leopold in 1853. An excellent timeline of anaesthesia can be found at **www.woodlibrarymuseum.org/history-of-anesthesia**.

The second problem, that of blood loss, meant that speed was essential in order to reduce the risk of the patient bleeding to death. Amputations, for example, had to be accomplished in three minutes if the patient was to survive. It was almost impossible to successfully amputate above the elbow or knee without the patient bleeding out. In the sixteenth century, French battlefield surgeon, Ambroise Paré, began to use ligatures to individually tie off blood vessels after an amputation. Although this was a vast improvement on cauterisation, he was unaware that the ligatures needed to be sterile, therefore infection set in.

The third problem was infection. It was not until 1862 that St Bartholomew's Hospital in London suggested that it was sensible for surgeons to wash their hands between autopsy and operation. Before then, individuals had occasionally put forward the idea that a hygiene regime might lower death rates but the response was derision and disbelief. It was Pasteur's Germ Theory that helped to convince surgeons that sterilising operating theatres and instruments was important. It was Joseph Lister who pioneered the concept of antiseptic surgery in the mid-nineteenth century. Until this time, the survival rate for operations was thought to be about 30 per cent. This figure represents those who left the operating table alive; it does not take account of deaths from infections that set in later. Initially, as surgical techniques improved, death rates increased. This was because more complex operations were attempted, resulting in more fatalities and what was known as the Black Period of Surgery in the mid-nineteenth century.

A discovery that had a significant impact on our ancestors' health was the development of antibiotics. It was not until after the Second World War that these became widely available, enabling the treatment of many illnesses and infections that might previously have proved fatal for our relatives.

Until the dissolution of the monasteries, in the 1530s, the religious houses had been the main providers of medical care. As the sixteenth and seventeenth centuries unfolded, the sick might be attended by a variety of personnel. The physician was university trained and highly respected. He was also very expensive, charging up to a week's wages for a working man, just for a consultation. His role was to diagnose and prescribe but not to dispense medications; that was the responsibility of the apothecary. The barber surgeon, who would perform any necessary operations, also required payment. Cure-all 'quack' medicines were on sale in the marketplace and Victorian newspapers carried advertisements for products that claimed to be effective for anything from gout to unwanted pregnancy. Until the advent of the National Health Service, in 1948, the cost of summoning a doctor would have been carefully considered and might have been prohibitive.

The housewife would be expected to be proficient in herbal lore and there were many curious 'treatments' that could be carried out at home. Our literate ancestresses might consult a herbal, such as those by Culpeper or Gerard. These would advise which plant, and which part of the plant, was appropriate for a particular ailment. Many women would be unable to read and would, therefore, have to garner this knowledge from their mothers and grandmothers, remember it and pass it on to the next generation.

The following are all recorded as being cures for plague. It is clear that their efficacy was limited and that, although unicorn horn might refer to a plant of that name, some might be difficult to procure.

- An ointment of egg yolk, honey and rue.
- Urinate on a mixture of yarrow, tansy and feverfew, then drink the strained liquid
- Make plague water from powdered unicorn horn and frogs' legs.
- Put the tail feathers of a chicken on the buboes to draw out the poison.
- Use a Bezoar stone.
- Make the victim sweat and lay a dead pigeon on the buboes.
- Place a dead toad on the neck.

From 1837, death certificates provide a cause of death, although some of these are imprecise – 'visitation of God' and 'old age' not being very informative. Before that, it is unusual to discover how individual ancestors died, or know what diseases they recovered from. Finding out about prevalent causes of death for those living in a particular era and being aware of the epidemics and illnesses that our ancestors would have feared, is, however, both feasible and informative. It is a welcome bonus if you find that a helpful clergyman noted a cause of death in a burial register. In the register for Frithelstock, Devon we learn that 'Honest John Palmer' was 'accidentally shot to death' on New Year's Day 1709. In the same parish, Jemima Ratcliffe, aged 20, died in 1797 'after amputation too long delayed of a white swelling in the knee'.

London Bills of Mortality were introduced in the late sixteenth century in order to monitor incidences of the plague. No names are listed but parish total numbers of christenings and burials are recorded, along with the parish clerk's assessment of the causes of death. These can often be very strange, such as 'horseshoehead'. The Bills were published weekly, with annual summaries. They provide evidence of what was accounting for London deaths at a particular time. For example, in 1775, 694 people died from 'Teeth' and 52 were described as 'Lunatick'. The Royal Society of Medicine Library **www.rsm.ac.uk/library/** has complete holdings of Bills of Mortality for 1657–1814.

In the days before health and safety awareness, many of our ancestors suffered from accidents in the course of their daily lives. Hazards abounded, machinery, tools, fires, modes of transport and animals were amongst the many potential causes.

In a few cases, specific information may be available. Some hospitals maintain their own archives, although there may be a restriction on access to more recent records. The Hospital Records' Database **www.nationalarchives.gov.uk/hospitalrecords**, a joint project between The National Archives and The Wellcome Medical Library, is part of The National Archives Discovery catalogue **https://discovery.nationalarchives.gov.uk** and will help with the location of records. The database can be searched by town or hospital name. Bristol Infirmary, for example, has admissions' books dating back to 1737. There is also a Voluntary Hospitals Database at **www.hospitalsdatabase.lshtm.ac.uk**. The Historical Hospital Admissions Records' Project **www.hharp.org** covers admissions' records between 1852 and 1921 for the Hospital for Sick Children at Great Ormond Street, the Evelina Hospital, the Alexandra Hospital for Children with Hip Disease in London and Glasgow's Royal Hospital for Sick Children. A list of hospitals and asylums, with the dates that they were founded, can be found in John Richardson's *The Local Historian's Encyclopaedia* (3rd ed. Historical Publications Ltd. 2003). The Lost Hospitals of London website **http://ezitis.myzen.co.uk** may also be helpful. It is well worth looking in local archives and making periodic checks at the main data-providing websites, searching for 'hospital' in their catalogues, to see what is available online.

Baptismal and admissions' records for 1749–1868 survive for the British Lying-in Hospital in Holborn. The original records are held by London Metropolitan Archives. The baptism registers are at The National Archives in class RG8, which can be searched on several online sites. Many of the patients were the wives of service personnel and they came from much further afield than just London. The Records for Chelsea and Greenwich Lying-in Hospitals are also in The National Archives.

First and Second World War medical records can be viewed at Findmypast; these are single line entries, referring to illnesses or wounds.

Images of the HMS *Dreadnought* Seaman's Hospital admissions' records from 1826 to 1920 are available on Ancestry. They give name, age, ship, rank, place of birth, illness, number of days in hospital and whether or not they were cured, relieved or discharged dead. Thomas Fidly, a 21-year-old able-bodied seaman from Hastings, from the ship *Amoret*, sailing from Sunderland to Whitstable, spent twenty-six days in hospital before being discharged to convalesce; he was suffering from venereal disease.

The admissions' records for several London workhouse infirmaries, covering the period 1842–1918, are held at London Metropolitan Archives and are also on Ancestry. These infirmaries were often the only place where poorer people could get medical treatment. For example, these records show that 4-year-old Maurice Axford was admitted to the infirmary in Mitcham, Surrey with a tubercular spine, having been transferred from Great Ormond Street Hospital.

Some of our families would have attempted to offset the cost of medical care and funeral costs by belonging to Friendly Societies or Death Clubs. They would make small, regular contributions in return for assistance in times of need. There were 27,000 such societies in nineteenth-century Britain. The Friendly Societies Act of 1829 imposed regulation, which in turn led to documentation and records may survive in county archives or, where they still exist, with the present-day society.

School log books, which might be found in local archives, frequently record outbreaks of illnesses, such as measles or scarlet fever, although they do not often name individual victims. School admissions' registers may note when and why a child on the school roll dies. Service records may also refer to ill-health and injuries acquired whilst serving in the armed forces.

The Public Health Act of 1848 introduced the role of the local Medical Officer of Health, each with responsibility for a Poor Law Union. They had to provide an annual report on conditions in their own areas. These give summaries of causes of death and report particular problems in the district. They may also mention severe weather conditions and public health problems. Copies of many annual reports are available on the internet archive **https://archive.org/details/medicalofficerofhealthreports**. Those for London boroughs from 1848 to 1972 are available at **http://wellcomelibrary.org/moh**. Some local newspapers summarised the reports.

From 1851 to 1911, the disability column of the census lists certain conditions. As mentioned in Chapter 1, in 1861, a survey was made of the 14,216 long-term adult workhouse inmates in England and Wales. These were individuals who had been continuously resident in the workhouse for five years or more, many of whom were sick or disabled in some way.

Disability could be a lifelong condition, or it might be the result of an accident or illness. Life-expectancy for all, but particularly the disabled, was much lower for our ancestors than it is now, with many disabled children not reaching adulthood. Some relatives with disabilities would have been cared for at home and might have been regarded with patronising tolerance by members of the community. Until comparatively recently, the prevailing view was that disability was a punishment from God, leading to both the disabled themselves and their parents being stigmatised. Those who were disabled, either physically or mentally, were regarded as a source of shame, family members who should be hidden away from society. This was largely due to the Biblical concept of 'sins of the fathers', whereby having a disabled child was seen to be indicative of moral defects in the character of the parents. Following the First World War, the many disabled ex-servicemen began to alter attitudes to the disabled but those with disabilities were still largely regarded as an embarrassment. Simon Jarrett's article, *Disability in Time and Place*, which is available on the Historic England website, is very informative on this topic **https://historicengland.org.uk/content/docs/research/disability-in-time-and-place-pdf/**.

In the 1320s, The Prerogativa Regis referred to those with a mental disability as follows:

> The king shall have ward of the lands of natural fools, taking the profits without waste or destruction, and shall find the necessaries; and after death of such idiots he shall render the estate to the heirs; in order to prevent such idiots from aligning their lands and their heirs from being disinherited.

Before the Reformation of the 1530s, the disabled, like the sick, were looked after in the community, or by the monastic houses. After the dissolution of the monasteries, the responsibility devolved to the parishes and secular private charities. Under the terms of the Elizabethan Poor Law, the disabled were classified as impotent poor. The Act reads:

> The person naturally disabled, either in wit or member, as an idiot, lunatic, blind, lame etc., not being able to work, all these are to be provided for by the overseers of necessary relief and are to have allowances according to their maladies and needs.

Thus, information about disabled family members might be found in the records of the overseers of the poor.

By the end of the eighteenth century, there was an increasing desire to institutionalise those who were incapacitated both physically and mentally. The creation of county asylums in the early nineteenth century catered for both the mentally ill and those with learning difficulties, often with little distinction between them and this is discussed in the next chapter. With the advent of the Poor Law Amendment Act of 1834, many disabled people became workhouse inmates.

In the nineteenth century, there was a belief that mental incapacity was reflected in an individual's facial features and cranial structure. The early twentieth century saw the rise of the Eugenics Movement, which advocated the sterilisation of what they termed the mentally enfeebled. This was not enshrined in law in Britain but was elsewhere. The 1913 Mental Deficiency Act introduced revised definitions for those with additional learning needs; it uses terms that are abhorrent today:

- Idiot – Those with IQs between 0 and 25, with poor motor skills, extremely limited communication and little response to stimulus. Those 'unable to guard themselves against physical danger'.
- Imbecile – Those with IQs between 26 and 50 who were unable to progress past a mental age of approximately six and 'incapable of managing themselves or their affairs'.
- Moron – Those with IQs between 51 and 70 who had adequate learning skills enabling them to complete menial tasks and to communicate.
- Feeble minded – anyone 'needing care or control for the protection of themselves or others'.
- Moral defective – those possessed of 'vicious or criminal propensities'.

There were certain institutions who specialised in the care of those with additional learning needs, although care was not always the principal aim; often, institutionalisation was more about the removal of those with disabilities from society's gaze. The Magdalen Hospital, Bath housed 'idiots' from the seventeenth century. In 1848, the National Asylum for Idiots opened in London; from 1863 it was based in Earlswood, Surrey and the records are held at Surrey Record Office.

An understanding of neurodiversity is very recent, with autism first being described in 1943 and the condition continuing to be under-diagnosed and imperfectly understood for decades after that. It is almost certain that relatives with neurodiverse conditions are part of most family trees; it is less likely that they can be identified. Those whose communication skills were severely impaired would have been categorised as 'idiots' and treated in the same way. Those with language skills may just have been regarded as misfits. Sadly, although it is next to impossible to identify them, some neurodiverse relatives would be likely to have fallen foul of the law and therefore appear in criminal records. It may be that family stories of more recent relatives are indicative of neurodiversity but without a medical diagnosis, this will remain speculation.

There are various useful resources about the history of disability on the Historic England website A History of Disability **https://historicengland.org.uk/research/inclusive-heritage/disability-history/**.

The Story of Richard Gill and William Leathern

In 1857, Richard Gill was born in Yarnscombe, Devon; his mother was 48. He was the eleventh and youngest child of George and Susan Gill née Martin. Only one of his older siblings died in infancy, suggesting that they were relatively healthy. Richard was privately baptised on 30 October 1858 in Yarnscombe. The fact that this baptism was both late and private could possibly be related to his condition. In the 1861 census, Richard was living in Yarnscombe with his parents and the three sisters closest to him in age, Selina, Lydia and Rebecca. His father, George, was described as a pauper invalid. Eight-year-old Selina was the only member of the household who was earning; she was making gloves on a piecework basis. Ten years later, all three daughters and their mother were glove-making. George, who was incorrectly enumerated with the forename Richard, was described as an annuitant. In this census, 13-year-old Richard had an entry in the disability column that reads 'imbecile'; a category that was not required to be recorded in earlier censuses. This suggests that Richard had significant additional learning needs and was unlikely to be capable of earning a living, or living independently. It is likely that Richard was stigmatised for his disability by some members of the community and that his family were also affected.

On 3 April 1876, at the age of 18, Richard died of convulsions; his death certificate records that he was a 'deformed imbecile'. A few weeks later, his older sister, Selina, was admitted into the county asylum, due, according to her admissions' record, to 'melancholia and nervous attack brought on by [the] death of [her] brother'. It is likely that Selina had taken on some of the day-to-day care of her disabled brother. After three years in the asylum, Selina returned to her home area and she married Eli Leathern, in 1880. The couple had three daughters, the youngest of whom died from whooping cough at the age of 2.

In 1891, Eli and Selina were living in rural Devon with their two surviving daughters. Eli was an agricultural labourer and Selina was still glove-making. She was heavily pregnant at this time and her son, William, was born a few months later.

The family belonged to the Bible Christian Church, an offshoot of Methodism that was popular in the South West. A few lines from a hymn book, used by the denomination, illustrates the atmosphere that the family would have encountered in chapel each Sunday.

> In that fearful day he'll seize thee
> Plunge thee in the burning lake.
> Think, poor sinner,
> Thine eternal all's at stake.'

It seems that Selina became uncomfortable in her faith and when William was 5, she was once again admitted to the asylum. She was recorded as 'incessantly talking', claiming she was lost and had 'sold herself to hell and cannot go to heaven'. This left Eli with three young children to bring up. In 1899, 8-year-old William was admitted to Torrington workhouse; he was described as an idiot. He is also recorded in the workhouse register of lunatics, illustrating the cross-over between mental illness and mental incapacity. Credit must be given to Eli for caring for William at home for three years without Selina's help. Was Selina's second breakdown related to William's disability? Did she feel outcast by her religious community because of her son's condition? The 1891 census for the workhouse gives further information; William was blind, deaf and dumb.

Was some genetic condition the cause of William's disability and that of his uncle Richard? An exploration of the wider family has not uncovered any further instances of disability. It is very difficult to assign a diagnosis with the minimal information available, but William's condition is not inconsistent with the effects of maternal Rubella during pregnancy. William died of pneumonia in 1905, when he was 14. His mother had died in the asylum, of tuberculosis, four years earlier.

Chapter 8

MENTAL ILL-HEALTH

Having considered how our ancestors were marginalised by physical ill-health and disability, it is time to think about those family members who struggled with their mental health. Although 'melancholia' was recognised as a condition, with specific mental and physical symptoms, as early as the fifth century BCE, it is only very recently that talking about mental ill-health has been encouraged. In the era when the theory of the four humours underpinned medical thinking, melancholia was thought to be the result of an excess of black bile. It was characterised not just by depression but was accompanied by delusions and fixations. In 1806, Pinel, in his book *A Treatise on Insanity*, described sufferers from melancholia as being 'overwhelmed by an exclusive idea, endlessly recalled in their words, which seems to absorb all their faculties'. He distinguishes this from idiocy, dementia and mania, describing the latter as a condition in which people exhibited 'nervous excitation or extreme restlessness, sometimes to the point of fury, and a variable level of general delusion'.

Sadly, being unable to manage the demands of daily life is not a new phenomenon. The stresses and anxieties of our ancestors may have been different to those of the twenty-first century but were no less significant. Compared with today, people of the past may have had lower expectations. They were free from media-fuelled peer pressure, but they might have been coping with poverty, hardship, insufficient leisure, a lack of privacy and the unremitting grind of working life. People worried about being unable to work because of illness or injury and faced the fear of epidemic diseases that were poorly understood and for which there were no effective preventatives or cures. For our rural ancestors, there was the constant worry that the weather would turn against them, the livestock might sicken, or the harvest fail. There were times of political unrest and conflict that would have been difficult to cope with, both for combatants and for those that they left behind. There may have been a climate of religious intolerance or even persecution to endure. Even though these conditions might have been regarded as the norm, they still took their toll.

Women could have been frustrated by the restrictions that they faced. Again, for the most part, this would have been accepted as just the way things were but there were still female ancestors who would have felt unfulfilled. In this regard, those further up the social scale in particular, might have resented their life of enforced idleness and lack of purpose. After the relative freedoms that women experienced during the First World War, when they deputised for fighting men, adjusting to the return to domesticity once peace came was difficult.

A significant factor for many of our forebears was a religious climate that was confining and often accompanied by fears of 'hellfire and damnation'. Adherence to a particular church or chapel went far beyond attending the Sunday service. An employer or landlord might have been someone with whom our ancestors worshipped, their social life revolved around their place of worship; religious convictions were all consuming. People took comfort in their beliefs and their certainty of a better place to come, an everlasting life in which they would be reunited with those who had gone before. Being part of a church or chapel community created a powerful sense of belonging. At the same time, commitment to a faith might impose a moral code that was difficult to live up to. The problems arose when an individual thought that they had stepped outside the embrace of the church, for whatever reason; not only did they feel completely isolated but they believed that they had imperilled their everlasting soul. Many asylum records list 'religious mania' as a reason for a patient's admission, together with comments such as, 'believes she cannot go to heaven', or, 'says he has sold his soul to the devil'. Selina's experience, outlined in the case study in the previous chapter, is a case in point. Non-conformity was associated with religious 'enthusiasm', including visions and speaking in tongues. This and even just vociferous preaching, might be equated with madness.

Mental illness was poorly understood, especially such conditions as post-natal depression and post-traumatic stress and it was usual to regard its occurrence as a cause for shame. There was often very little sympathy for sufferers, who would be encouraged to 'pull themselves together'. Mental illness, like mental or physical disability, was often regarded as a punishment from God. Insanity might be blamed on the actions of the sufferer's mother during pregnancy. There was also a concept of moral insanity, which led to promiscuity being equated with madness. This extended to what were regarded as moral lapses such as masturbation, having an illegitimate child, or even marrying an 'unsuitable' person, all of which might have been seen as grounds for incarceration in an asylum.

It is important to distinguish between those with learning difficulties, who might have been described, in language that is no longer acceptable, as 'idiots' or 'imbeciles' and the mentally ill. The latter were usually labelled 'lunatics' because of the perceived association between madness and the phases of the moon. The neurodivergent might be categorised in any of these ways. Historically, attitudes towards, and the treatment of, the mentally ill and those with additional learning needs were often blurred, especially before the 1845 Lunatics' Act established, somewhat crude, definitions for various classifications of mental disability. This act also deemed that hearsay was not sufficient grounds for admitting someone to an asylum. The family's opinion would be sought, but Justices of the Peace had to receive a doctor's certificate and then make orders to admit a patient. The certifying doctors could not be one of the asylum's medical officers, as they would have a conflict of interest.

How can a family historian identify the mentally ill amongst their ancestors? There may be stories about an auntie who suffered with her 'nerves', of family members who had a breakdown, or even accounts of those who were institutionalised, but the taboo surrounding mental illness often means that there is no legacy in the oral accounts. From 1871 to 1911, the disability column of the British census returns includes scope for recording 'lunatics' and such an entry may be the first clue that all was not well. Death certificates also reveal deaths from what we would now recognise as dementia. This may be recorded as 'senile decay', or some such similar term, although senile decay might also refer to a physical condition. There may be mentions of 'melancholia', or irrational behaviour, in service records, as individuals found it difficult to cope with life in the armed forces.

If mental illness ended tragically, in suicide, this will be recorded, either starkly or more guardedly, on the death certificate. Occasionally, there are references to suicides in burial registers. The register for Wylye, Wiltshire in 1773 reads, 'Jane Compton July 28th the said Jane Compton laid or lent hands upon herself and therefore no tolling of the Bell nor reading of the Burial Service at her funeral.'

Suicide will have been followed by a coroner's inquest. Sadly, inquest records themselves do not survive well, although it is always worth checking in local archives just in case. The press coverage of an inquest, however, can be extensive and include verbatim witness statements. Even unsuccessful suicide attempts might be reported. Suicide was, of course, a crime in the eyes of both the state and the church and would not have been resorted to lightly. Suicide was illegal in Britain until 1961. Those who took their own lives could not be buried in consecrated ground until

1823 and then only without the benefits of a religious service. Full burial rights for those who took their own lives were not officially granted by the Church of England until 2015, although some clergy ignored, or seemed to be unaware of, this limitation. This means that there may be no burial record. If someone in the family took their own life, it would probably have been hushed up if possible. General paralysis of the insane is sometimes recorded as a cause of death on a certificate. This is the result of long-term, untreated, or imperfectly treated, syphilis and is likely to have meant that the sufferer was committed to an asylum.

Finally, there are the asylum records themselves. Until fairly recently, a researcher would be unlikely to consult these unless they had a suspicion that they might contain details of a family member. Now that some admissions' registers are being made available online, a general search for an individual on one of the data-providing websites might lead to an asylum record. This could be the first indication that a family member was struggling with their mental health. Any indicators of mental ill-health should prompt the researcher to seek out further information, such as asylum records, for the appropriate area. Even if your own family do not seem to have suffered, it is worth looking at asylum case books to gain an impression of the attitudes of the time.

The most notorious asylum is Bethlem (a corruption of Bethlehem) Royal Hospital in London, from whose name the word 'bedlam' derives. It opened its doors in the thirteenth century and from 1407, became known for taking in those who were deemed to be 'mad'. Do not think, because this was a London hospital, that all its inmates were from the south-east. Individuals from all over the country can be found in its records, which are held at The National Archives. These include Admissions' Registers for 1683–1932; Minutes of the Court of Governors 1559–1689; Incurable Patient Admissions' Registers 1723–1919; and Discharge and Death Books for 1782–1906. The Admissions' Registers and Case Books can be accessed on Findmypast. There is more information about the archives of Bethlem Hospital on its website **https://museumofthemind.org.uk**.

The most revealing of the Bethlem Hospital records are the Patient Case Books, which date from 1815 to 1919. These give information about the name, address, occupation, age and religion of the patients. In addition, they provide details of the background medical history and symptoms; sometimes there is also a physical description. There are observations from two doctors and members of the family, followed by details of the patient's progress. Frequently quoted symptoms in the case books include incessant talking, inappropriate laughter or singing, religious mania, neglecting children, irrational fears, swearing or blaspheming and persecution complexes.

From the sixteenth to nineteenth centuries, those deemed to be insane may have been incarcerated in the village lock-up, managed within the community, or sent to private institutions. Here they would be under the supervision of a 'mind doctor' or 'alienist'. The Madhouses Act of 1774 brought in a system of licensing and inspection of private asylums. If they were found to be admitting the sane whose families wanted rid of them, a not uncommon way of removing an unwanted

The Lunatic Asylum, *unknown engraver, image in the public domain, accessed via Wikimedia Commons.*

family member, then the licence could be refused. Nonetheless, in 1845, Richard Paternoster felt the need to found the Alleged Lunatics Friends' Society, after he was incarcerated, he felt unjustly, by his father. This organisation was superseded in 1873 by the Lunacy Law Reform Association.

'Treatments' included restraint using manacles and straight-jackets; drugging with laudanum; putting patients in an insulin-induced coma; and hypnosis. As mental illness might be regarded as possession, exorcisms were carried out. Surgical treatments included castration, mutilation, trepanning and attempting to transfuse animal blood into the patient. Benjamin Rush, regarded as the father of American psychiatry, advocated more humane treatments in the Pennsylvanian hospital where he worked. He believed that mental illness was caused by disruptions of the circulation. He therefore attempted to improve the circulation to the brain by encouraging the patient to spin, in order to settle the disordered nerves and by using devices such as the Tranquilliser Chair. This would scarcely be regarded as humane today. Galvanism, a form of electric shock treatment, was thought to be beneficial to those who were suffering mentally. From 1938, electroconvulsive therapy was used.

There were also various herbal remedies that were recommended for mental illness. Ground primrose root was advised for nervous disorders, particularly amongst women; melancholia was treated with the berries of St John's Wort. Buttercups were nicknamed 'crazy' and were worn hidden in a hessian bag round the neck to prevent madness. Doctor Wadenfield's cure for lunacy was recorded by Mary Kettilby, in her recipe book of 1734. It involved shredding three handfuls of ground ivy (a member of the nettle family) and boiling it in 2 quarts of white wine. Six ounces of best salad oil were to be added to the reduced, strained mixture. The warm ointment was then to be rubbed on the patient's shaved head. In addition, unspecified fresh herbs were to be bound to the patient's head and three spoonfuls of ground ivy, mixed with beer, were to be drunk each day for ten days. Wadenfield claimed that this remedy had cured sixty patients. John Gerard, writing in 1633, stated that borage flowers and leaves 'put in to wine make men and women glad and merry, driving away all sadness, dulnesse and melancholy'. It is debatable how much of this was due to the borage and how much to the wine.

The 1808 County Asylums Act gave Justices of the Peace the authority to build county lunatic asylums but not all counties did so straight away; it was 1845 before this became compulsory. The new asylums were to be 'fixed in a healthy situation', built on high ground with clean air. The facilities were to include a kitchen garden, a chapel, workshops, a

Casa de Locos, *Francisco Goya c.1817, image in the public domain, accessed via Wikimedia Commons.*

laundry and living quarters for the senior staff. They were to be powered by their own gas works and sited near a railway. Men and women were housed separately, in dormitories for between eight and fifteen patients. The sick, those who might harm others and those awaiting discharge, had single rooms.

Attitudes to the mentally ill began to change in the early nineteenth century. In earlier times it was considered acceptable to open asylums to paying visitors and exhibit the inmates for 'entertainment'. By the Victorian era, there was less emphasis on restraint and more on the treatment of those who could be helped and the care of those who could not. Scientific thinking gradually replaced superstition and the insane were less likely to be regarded as having been possessed or cursed. The nineteenth century saw a significant increase in the number of people being diagnosed as lunatics, reaching 1 in 400 by the end of the century. It seems likely that this escalation in cases was, at least in part, due to a rising population and an increased awareness.

A good starting point, when researching your mentally ill family members, is The National Archives' research guide *Asylums, Psychiatric Hospitals and Mental Health* **www.nationalarchives.gov.uk/help-with-your-research/research-guides/mental-health/**. The National Archives holds records of the Office of Commissioners in Lunacy. These include admissions' registers for the asylums and psychiatric hospitals of the Lunacy Commission and Board of Control, dating from 1846 to 1960, in class MH94. Those for the period up to 1921 can be viewed on Ancestry.

The information includes the patient's name and the date of admission and discharge to the specified institution. There are annotations to show if the patients recovered, were relocated, had not improved, or if they died. On some records, there are details of whether the individual was a private patient or a pauper.

Criminal Lunacy and Warrant Entry Books for 1882–1898 are also held at The National Archives in class HO145; these too are available on Ancestry. The Criminal Lunatic Asylum Registers, kept by the National Lunatic Asylum and county and metropolitan asylums, are in class HO20 at The National Archives and cover the period 1800–1843. These contain a wealth of detail about those who had been convicted of criminal offences but were deemed to be insane. The entry for Ann Palmer, from Dagenham, Essex, who was convicted of murder at Chelmsford Assizes in 1823, is a good example. Ann, in a state of grief, had killed her 11-month-old son, Thomas:

> The jury having found that she was insane at the time of the commission of the offence declare that she was acquitted by them on account of such insanity.
> From Dagenham, Essex.
>
> Previous to Commitment. About 25 years since she partially cut her throat while she lived as a servant at Newington. Is said to have been a good and affectionate mother. Was married to a very afflicted man who kept a small public house at Marks Gate, Padnell Corner, Dagenham and became much afflicted in her mind at her husband's death, which happened a short time before her commitment in consequence of her being informed that his body had been stolen from the grave.
>
> Conduct in gaol since. Decidedly insane, sometimes violent, at others dull and moody but not dangerous to those about her.
> Thos. Cawkivell Gaoler, Jas. Hutchinson Chaplain.
>
> The state of her bodily health varied much during the period of her confinement but more particularly since the time of her trial. She was at one time reduced to so feeble a state that considerable apprehensions were entertained of her probable dissolution but she has within the last 10 or 12 days become more tranquil and has appeared gradually to acquire a strength insomuch that I have no hesitation in pronouncing her capable of safe removal to any place which may be appointed for her.
>
> 14 August 1823 G.A. Gepp Surgeon.

Ann died on 23 February 1824.

Both Ancestry and Findmypast provide access to some records relating to specific asylums and hospitals. Records of lunatics in the care of the Chancery Courts are also at The National Archives. These relate to wealthy lunatics who were deemed to be incapable of managing their own affairs, so the Chancery Court administered their property.

North of the border, the General Register of Lunatics in Asylums is held by National Records of Scotland and covers the period 1858–1978 but includes records of patients who were admitted prior to 1858 and were still in the asylum at that date. There is a 100-year closure rule on these records.

There are other institutions that have surviving records. For example, from 1818, the East India Company ran its own asylum for employees at Pembroke House in Mare Street, Hackney. The Hospital Records Database on the National Archives website at **www.nationalarchives.gov.uk/hospitalrecords** says that:

> The East India Company made arrangements to send any of its servants who became insane while in India back to Britain and to lodge them with Dr George Rees of Pembroke House, Hackney. The Company paid Dr Rees £40 a year for each soldier, sailor or minor civil servant (second-class patients) and £100 a year for officers and senior civil servants (first-class patients). Although patients were expected to reimburse the Company from their pension or other income, in practice the Company subsidised many of the second-class patients. It was sold in 1870 and the India Office acquired the Elm Grove estate, Ealing, and set about converting the house there to receive patients.

The armed forces also established hospitals to care for military personnel who were unwell; this would include those who might otherwise have been admitted to an asylum. Those in the navy would be sent to Haslar Hospital in Gosport on the south coast, whilst those in the army went to the nearby Royal Victoria Hospital in Netley, Hampshire. The thinking behind the location of these hospitals was that those returning by sea from a theatre of war would not have far to travel once on British soil. The National Archives hold records relating to patients and staff at Haslar. These include admission and discharge records from 1795–1957 and clinical and patient records from 1787 to 1899. There are a few records for Netley at the Wellcome Institute Library **https://wellcomecollection.org** but most of these relate to administration not patients. Patient records cover 1863–1883 only. Records for Broadmoor, the prison for the criminally insane, which opened in 1864, are at The National Archives.

Quaker William Tuke founded The Retreat in York in 1792, to care for the mentally ill. This was not set up as an institution where sufferers could be removed from society. Instead, it was what Tuke called a 'retired habitation', with a focus on patient care, an attitude that was untypically enlightened for the time. Its records are at The Borthwick Institute **https://borthcat.york.ac.uk**.

Surviving county asylum records are normally found in local archives, although a 100-year closure rule applies to documents that refer to named patients. It is well worth using Ancestry's card catalogue and the equivalent 'all record sets' at Findmypast and searching for 'asylum' and 'lunacy', to see what records they hold. Those with mental health conditions might end up in the workhouse, if only temporarily, so do search their records too. In 1815, parish overseers of the poor sent lists of pauper lunatics to the Clerk of the Peace and these will be with records of the Quarter Sessions' Courts in county record offices.

Doctors often ask patients if there is any history of a particular disease in the family; as with some physical complaints, the propensity to depression and mental ill-health can run in families. If we find that our own ancestry includes those who have spent time in asylums, or who have taken their own lives, how do we feel about this? Does it make us more uncomfortable than finding out, for example, that several ancestors suffered from heart disease? We are encouraged to talk about our own mental ill-health and we can be empathetic to those members of our family who suffered in times when mental illness was little understood. Let us discuss their difficulties freely and honour their memory.

The Story of Fanny Amelia Ellington
Fanny Amelia was baptised at St Michael's, Highgate on 5 March 1848, the daughter of Philip and Mary Woolgar née Cardell. Although Fanny outlived her brother and two sisters, Caroline and Mary Ann, there were no family recollections of her. There was, however, a vague suggestion that Philip and Mary had a daughter, Sophie, so there was some awareness that there may have been a third daughter, even if her name was incorrect.

On 15 November 1884, Fanny Amelia married widower, William Ellington, at St Clement's, Hastings, Sussex. William was inconsistent about his age and place of birth but the consensus seems to be that he was born about 1823 in Peterborough, so he was 61, not 52 as the marriage certificate claimed. He was considerably older than Fanny and she was younger than some of his children.

William and Fanny Ellington's son, George Frederick, was born in Hastings a year after they married. There was another son, Richard Collings Stanley Ellington, who was born in 1891 and died the following year. In the 1891 census, the family was living in two rooms in part of 19 Cornfield Terrace, Hastings and William was working as a bathchair man, wheeling about those who visited Hastings to take the air. Although no death registration has been found for William Ellington, by 1911, Fanny was a widow and in the census, can be found visiting the Pierpoint family in Dulwich, just outside London and close to the homes of her siblings. No family relationship has been found to the Pierpoints.

On 2 May 1911, just weeks after the census was taken, Fanny was admitted to the workhouse in Constance Road, East Dulwich, because she was 'allegedly insane'; she was discharged a week later, to Horton Asylum, described as being 'destitute'. Horton Asylum, in Epsom, Surrey, was to become noted for pyrotherapy, an experimental treatment for the general paralysis of the insane. This treatment involved infecting the sufferers with malaria. It was thought that the resulting high fever would destroy the syphilis. Horton was deemed suitable as it had an isolation unit, which would prevent the malaria spreading to other patients. It seems that the procedure was pioneered in 1917, so Fanny would have escaped this treatment as she had left by then.

There are two entries for Fanny in the MH94 Lunacy Commission Registers. The first relates to her admission to Horton on 9 May 1911. It states that she was a pauper and that she was discharged on 12 July 1911, being relocated. The Horton Asylum records also substantiate this. They record her as a 61-year-old widow from Camberwell, with no occupation and note that it was her first attack. The medical register reveals that she had been unwell for a month and was suffering from mental stress, senility and cardiovascular degeneration. Her form of insanity was said to be 'recent melancholia'.

The second entry in the Lunacy Commission registers shows that she was admitted to East Sussex's Hellingly Asylum on 12 July 1911 and was discharged 'recovered' on 4 October in the same year. This would have been the asylum for Hastings and indicates that Hastings was still regarded as Fanny's home area. The Female Patients' Index Register for East Sussex Asylum confirmed the dates of admission and discharge given in the Lunacy Commission Registers. It also notes that Eastbourne Poor Law Union was responsible for her support. The East Sussex Asylum Patient Case Books provide not only a detailed medical history but also two photographs. Fanny's records reads:

> Talks and behaves quite rationally but knows that she has been off her head and imagined she was very wicked; she does not know what put such an idea into her mind but supposes she has been run down and her mind affected for some six months. She has

not slept well but did better the first night she was here and had natural sleep. She admits that she hears voices telling her to swear.

Fanny's diagnosis was 'delusional insanity'. Her medical history also reveals that she had had rheumatic fever and had suffered a head injury as a child. Anxiety, poverty and an operation were regarded as factors contributing to her condition.

On 30 December 1915, according to the workhouse admissions' register, Fanny was readmitted to the Constance Road Workhouse from 18 Hindmans Road. In 1911, this had been the home of a younger generation of the Pierpoint family. Once again, she was regarded as being 'allegedly insane' and 'destitute'. Workhouses were supposed to transfer inmates to asylums swiftly, if this was deemed appropriate, and after six days Fanny was removed to Cane Hill Pauper Lunatic Asylum in Coulsdon, Surrey. At this time, Horton had been requisitioned for military use. She appears in the admissions' register for Cane Hill, which is held at Croydon Archives, but no patient records have been located.

Fanny Ellington died in Cane Hill Asylum on 12 January 1922 from valvular disease of the heart and congestion of the lungs, both of an indefinite duration, hours after suffering a small cerebral haemorrhage. The death was registered by her son, George, who was then of 2 Grove Road, Chertsey, Surrey. There was no mention of Fanny's mental state. She is not recorded as having been buried in the asylum.

Cane Hill Asylum, postcard from the collection of Janet Few.

Chapter 9

THE ROMANY AND TRAVELLER COMMUNITY

Members of the Roma, or Romany and Traveller community were not only marginalised but also itinerant, therefore doubly difficult to trace. An ingrained wariness of officialdom means that the Romany people may be under-represented in some records, such as birth registrations and census returns. Conversely, they may feature more frequently than average in settlement and court records, as well as in newspaper reports of trials.

It is not always easy to identify those of Romany origin. There may be family stories of Gypsy ancestry. These may indeed have a basis in truth but, equally, can be romanticised fantasies. There are certain surnames that are typically found amongst the Romany people: Boswell, Smith, or the Romany equivalent Petulengro, Lee, Lovell, Loveridge, Gray/Grey, Faw, Buckland, Penfold/Pinfold and Cooper, for example. It is important to remember that many people with these surnames are not of Romany descent. The use of aliases is common amongst Romanies, and families frequently took the surname of the wife or mother, or would alternate between more than one surname. So, amongst other examples, we find the Heron family using the name Young and the Mobbs family becoming Gray. Romanies usually married within the family group, leading to complex, intertwined genealogies.

Unusual forenames might also be found, such as, for females, Aquilla, Cinderella, Parthena or Sinfi, and for males, Adolphus, Bendigo, Elisha, Napoleon, Sylvanus or Wisdom. Typically, Romany forenames include some more obscure biblical names and names that reflect the child's birthplace. Again, these names can also be found in non-Romany families. If aliases, or surname changes, make it difficult to trace a Romany family, the use of unusual forenames can be an advantage. It is possible to search for a combination of forenames in a census, rather than for a surname and this may reveal the family with an alternative last name.

Certain occupations might also be a clue to Romany heritage. Look out for tinkers, hawkers (who were traditionally on horseback), pedlars (who were on foot), horse dealers, basket-makers, musicians, peg-makers and seasonal workers, such as hop-pickers. Itinerancy is indicative of Traveller families and children are likely to have been born in different places. It is important to understand that the itinerancy was not haphazard. Families often followed set routes, frequented a regular cycle of fairs and markets and overwintered in established camping grounds or Gypsyries. These grounds might be identifiable from place names such as Gypsy Hill.

First printed in 1769, William Owen's *Book of Fairs* was later reprinted as the New Book of Fairs. Its full title gives a flavour of its contents:

> Owen's *(New) Book of Fairs*, published by the King's Authority. Being an authentic account of all the fairs in England and Wales, as they have been settled to be held since the alteration of the stile. Noting likewise the commodities which each of the said fairs is remarkable for furnishing; also the days on which markets are respectively held; with the distances from London; and the number of members which each place sends to Parliament.

Editions may be available as facsimiles.

Pat Loveridge's *Calendar of Fairs and Markets*, available from the Romany and Traveller Family History Society, provides clues regarding which markets Romany ancestors may have attended. Directories will also give information about local markets; remember to look out for fairs specialising in certain products, horse fairs in particular.

Although Romany families are more likely than the general population to escape enumeration in the census, addresses that mention 'living in a tent', or 'camping on the common', are further indicators that a family might be Travellers. Not all those enumerated in this way were Romanies and equally, some Romany families became settled and might be found living in houses.

As Sharon Floate points out, in her excellent *My Ancestors were Gypsies*, you need several of the factors mentioned above in a family before you strongly suspect Romany heritage.

It is important to distinguish between English and Welsh Romanies and Celtic Travellers, with Scottish and Irish origins, who are separate ethnic groups. The Irish Travellers, diverged from the settled Irish population and arrived in mainland Britain in the nineteenth century. They sometimes appear in the records as Mincéirs, or Pavees. In Scotland, the

Traveller community is diverse. Highland Travellers, or Ceàrdannan, are another ethnically distinct group. There is a Celtic Traveller DNA project and more about these communities can be found at **www.familytreedna.com/groups/celtic-traveller/about/background**. This webpage also contains a long list of Romany and non-Romany Traveller surnames.

Fairground people and showmen are not ethnically Romany and having fairground ancestors is not synonymous with Romany heritage, but there is some overlap between the communities and many of the same records and search techniques apply.

The general migration westward across Europe in the fifteenth century included the Roma or Romanichal people, who were colloquially referred to as 'Egyptians' or Gypsies. They were so called because they were believed to have originated, not in Egypt but in a region of the Peloponnese (now Greece) known as Little Egypt. In fact, they had come from further east, in India and travelled via Persia to the Balkans and then to western Europe, including Britain. They were first recorded in Scotland in 1505,

Irish Travellers' Decorated Caravan. National Library of Ireland, accessed via Wikimedia Commons (6136023633).

when the king paid a group of Egyptians £7. Ten years later, they were also noted in England. It is possible that early arrivals travelled as pilgrims on a penitential journey and as such would have been granted safe passage but most would be working as tinkers or hawkers and also as entertainers.

Despite the usefulness of Romany pedlars of ironmongery and basketware and their skills as craftspeople and entertainers, various factors led to discrimination and marginalisation. At a time of increasing poverty, there was a general unease surrounding vagrancy, which was associated with social unrest. Aspects of the Romany lifestyle were equated with begging, which was equally feared and frowned upon. In addition, fortune telling offended religious principles and might be likened to witchcraft.

In the sixteenth century, general legislation outlawing vagrancy and begging, such as the 1536 Act for the Punishment of Sturdy Vagabonds and Beggars, was accompanied by laws that specifically targeted 'Egyptians'. The Egyptians' Act of 1530 described the Romany people as:

> an outlandish People, calling themselves Egyptians, using no Craft nor Feat of Merchandise, who have come into this Realm, and gone from Shire to Shire, and Place to Place, in great Company; and used great, subtil, and crafty Means to deceive the People; bearing them in Hand that they, by Palmistry, could tell Men's and Women's Fortunes, and so many Times by Craft and

Gypsies Fortune Telling from the Robert Dawson Romani Collection, used under Creative Commons CC BY-SA 4.0, accessed via Wikimedia Commons.

> Subtilty have deceived the People of their Money, and also have committed many heinous Felonies and Robberies, to the great Hurt and Deceit of the People that they have come among. ... The Egyptians now being in this realm, have monition to depart within sixteen days ... from henceforth no such person be suffered to come within this the King's realm and if they do, then they and every of them so doing, shall forfeit to the King our Sovereign Lord all their goods and titles and then to be commanded to avoid the realm within fifteen days under pain of imprisonment.

Thus, anyone designated as an Egyptian was ordered to leave within sixteen days or forfeit their possessions. This did not include those who had been born in England, or who had arrived in England from Scotland, so this law was amended by an act of 1554, which made being a Gypsy an offence that might attract a capital penalty. This act remained on the statute books until 1783. In 1562, the legislation was extended beyond the Romany ethnic group to include 'counterfeit Egyptians', whose lifestyle replicated that of the Romanies. Under the terms of Elizabethan Poor Law, Romanies were regarded as the undeserving poor.

In 1656, Oliver Cromwell ordered all vagrants with no means of support to be transported to the Americas. The Romany community was adversely affected by the settlement legislation of 1662, which required all newcomers to a parish to undergo a settlement examination, in order to determine which parish would be responsible if they required poor relief. This same legislation fuelled suspicions of strangers and led to hostility against incomers who might become chargeable on the parish. Persecution continued in the nineteenth century with the 1822 Turnpike Roads Act, which imposed fines of £2 for camping on the roadside of turnpike roads. The 1824 Vagrancy Act, which made it an offence to sleep rough, also specifically mentioned fortune tellers.

As noted above, their itinerant lifestyle makes Romany families difficult to trace, as does the propensity for using aliases. They may appear in the standard records, such as parish registers. There was a tendency to baptise, rather than register births, but baptisms often did not take place in the location of birth and might be in batches, with several children in a family being baptised together. The census was taken at a time of year when Romany people were on the move, making it more likely that they were not enumerated. Even after education was made compulsory, Traveller children may have escaped. It was not until the 1908 Education Act that the requirement for compulsory education was extended to the children of nomadic parents. From then on, Romany children would have had to attend at least 200 school sessions (half-days) each year, which amounted to half-time education.

Romany Vardo of the English Gypsies early twentieth century. Image in the public domain, accessed via Wikimedia Commons.

School admissions' registers will note the frequent entrances and exits of children from Romany families, often with the same children returning for a few weeks each year.

From 1697, badgers or kidders, who sold grain, higglers who sold corn and other foodstuffs and drovers, all had to be licensed by the Quarter Session Courts but many from within the Romany community who carried out these occupations would have avoided this requirement. From 1870, the police assumed the responsibility for issuing licences. Quarter Sessions Courts were also responsible for many criminal trials and Romanies and other Travellers might be found being tried for vagrancy, or crimes such as petty theft, in these and other courts. Newspaper reports of court proceedings can be the best place to find clues that a trial took place.

Anyone with suspected Romany and Traveller ancestry should make full use of the resources of the Romany and Traveller Family History Society **http://rtfhs.org.uk**. The Gypsy Lore Society was founded in 1888 and is now based in the US. There is online access to many of their journals **https://catalog.hathitrust.org/Record/000499763**. The Robert Dawson Collection is housed at the Museum of English Rural Life in Reading, Berkshire **https://merl.reading.ac.uk/collections/robert-dawson-romany-collection/** and the National Fairground and Circus Archive is held by the University of Sheffield Fairground Heritage Trust **www.fairground-heritage.org.uk**.

The Story of Joshua Mobbs

Joshua Mobbs and his family first came to light in the 1881 census, as the inhabitants of a house in Chapman Street, Market Rasen, Lincolnshire. Other research into the history of this street established that they lived at number 10, a Victorian end-of-terrace house, next door to the local vagrants' ward. At this stage, there was little to suggest that they were a Romany family. Joshua, claiming to be aged 48, was a labourer and living with his wife Harriet, four sons and two daughters. The children did have rather unusual names, including sons Lasher, Anice and Uriah and a daughter Raney. All the family were born in Lincolnshire and with four of the six children having been born in Market Rasen, or neighbouring Middle Rasen, they did not seem to be unusually itinerant. A report in the *Lincolnshire Chronicle* of 12 October 1883 stated that a Chapman Street property in the occupation of Mrs Rosetta Smith sold for £40, when it had previously been worth £90, because 'it has lately been inhabited by a gypsy family, who allowed it to get into a dilapidated state.' There did not, at this point, seem to be anything to connect Mrs Smith to Joshua Mobbs, although subsequent research revealed that there was a relationship, as will be seen.

It was relatively straightforward to find members of the family in the 1891 census, enumerated as Mobs. Joshua, Harriet and four of the children were amongst twenty-three inhabitants of Jubilee Lodging House, 31 Waterside Lane South in Lincoln. The occupation of the whole family was given as Pedlar (Hawker) and Raney had become Emily. Unfortunately, it has not been possible to find out anything further about this institution. Going back in time to 1871 proved to be more difficult, especially as Joshua was now claiming to be two years older than he had been a decade later. The family was located by focusing on Uriah and looking for anyone with a forename beginning with U born about 1868 living in or near Market Rasen. This brought up Urky Gray. Apart from Joshua's age, the ages and birthplaces of what was now the Gray family, were similar enough to the Mobbs, to clearly be the same family with a change of surname. Two new, older, sons were present, William and Moses. Lasher had become Elijah, Anice was now Reajiel and Raney/Emily was recorded as Renky. They were living in Serpentine Street, Market Rasen and Joshua was described as a labourer.

Baptisms have been located for some of the children, using the surname Gray and there are birth registrations as Gray for three of the younger children, where the mother's maiden name is given as Brown. Joshua Mobs [sic] married Harriet Smith in 1876, at least twenty-four years after the birth of their oldest child. A ninth and final, short-lived, child was born after their marriage and registered with the surname Mobbs and the mother's maiden name Smith. There is nothing to suggest that

Joshua had children with two different women, both called Harriet and both born about 1836 in Blyborough. It seemed that Harriet Smith and Harriet Brown were one and the same and further research showed that this was indeed the case.

It is the 1861 census that strongly suggested that this was a Romany family. Joshua, Harriet and two sons were living in Reepham, Lincolnshire as part of an extended family group of Mobbs, Browns, Smiths and Grays. Joshua was a clothes-peg maker and other occupations included chair-bottomers and a musician. It seems that the 1860s marked Joshua's transition to a more static way of life.

The local newspapers provide evidence of Joshua being accused of a series of minor offences. In February 1881, the *Stamford Mercury* revealed that Joshua Mobbs, a labourer of Market Rasen, was fined 10 shillings and costs, or alternatively was to spend fourteen days in prison, for moving nine sheep from North Willingham to Market Rasen without a licence. The *Lincolnshire Chronicle* of 9 August 1881 reported that Joshua was fined for obtaining half a loaf of bread, ½lb of cheese and ½oz of tobacco, worth a total of 10½d, under false pretences. This offence is reported in the Criminal Registers, which are held in class HO27 at The National Archives. They show that Joshua received one month's imprisonment with hard labour. The Calendar of Prisoners refers to a previous offence, in 1880, when the theft of a hoe had led to seven days in prison.

In May the following year, Joshua was again in trouble, this time for not sending his son Charles to school. Joshua claimed that this was because the boy was suffering from 'the foreign itch'. Despite witnesses reporting that they had seen the child out playing, it was found that Charles did indeed have the itch and Joshua escaped being fined. Just two months later, Joshua Mobbs aka John Gray of Market Rasen, an 'old offender' was committed for trial at the October Quarter Sessions for taking three eggs from Mr Rigall of Glenworth. This time the Calendar of Prisoners states that Joshua, a chair-mender, was sentenced to six weeks in prison.

Joshua's wife, Harriet, died in 1897 and is buried in Scartho Road Cemetery, Grimsby but no death or burial has been found for Joshua. With a possible alias of John Gray this is not surprising.

Further investigation into the entwined and much inter-married, Mobbs, Gray, Smith and Brown families revealed that Joshua and Harriet were first cousins once removed, both descending from the notorious Wisdom Smith. Harriet's mother was the Rosetta Smith who had left the Chapman Street house in a state of disrepair. Were the family housed there as an overspill from the neighbouring vagrants' ward perhaps? Wisdom Smith, 1763–1839, was styled 'The Gypsy King'. He was associated with the rural poet John Clare who wrote a series of poems about Gypsy life, allegedly inspired by Wisdom.

A press report on members of the Boswell family, who were related to the Mobbs by marriage, provides a good illustration of the itinerant way of life. On 28 November 1853, the publication *John Bull* reported as follows:

> A Royal Family in Trouble. On Saturday the Retford Bench of Magistrates had four members of a Royal family placed before them, three of whom they sent to the tread-mill for a month, and committed the other for trial on a charge of felony. The illustrious prisoners, who trace their descent from a long line of ancestors, were Elijah Boswell, King of the Gipsies, and three of his sons. The following is an account of the Royal family from the pen of the Court newsman:- 'The King has been married three times, and has issue:- 1. Eliza, born among the ling in Mansfield forest; 2. Henrietta born in Thieves-dale-lane near Osberton; 3. Alfred, born in Treswell Back-lane; 4. Walter, born on Kneesall-green; 5. Adelaide, born in a lane between Langwith and Plessley; 6. Henry, born in a lane near West Stockwith; 7. Lucy, born under Firbeck-park-side; 8. Adam, born on Walesby Breck; 9. William, born in Gamston-wood; 10. James, born in Layard's Leap, between Newark and Sleaford; 11. Elijah, born near Sturton Highhouse; 12. Magnus, born in a lane near Langford; 13. Riley, born near Bole guide-post; 14. Alice, born in a lane near Mattersey Gorse.

Chapter 10

WITCHCRAFT

This chapter contains descriptions of methods of torture that some readers may find distressing.

Superstition lingers on in modern British society. Seeing a black cat might be viewed as being lucky, whereas breaking a mirror might not. For our sixteenth- and seventeenth-century ancestors, superstition was a way of life; they lived during an era when there was an overriding belief in, and fear of, witchcraft. Citing witchcraft was a way of making sense of inexplicable events in a chaotic world. In times of adversity, when sickness or disaster befell, the finger of suspicion might point towards marginalised members of the community. This was an atmosphere in which a whispered suspicion might, under the influence of peer pressure, escalate into mass hysteria. Once witchcraft was mooted, in order to avoid being accused, our ancestors could find themselves as accusers. Of course, many would be neither alleged victim, accuser, witness, nor accused, yet they might still be fearful of being caught up in witchcraft accusations in one role or another. As Martin Gaskill, in his book *Witchfinders: A Seventeenth Century English Tragedy* wrote, 'Witchcraft suspicions tend to move in an ever-widening ripple through the village, the final accusation being based on a general consensus of opinion which rested on the mutual exchange of fears through gossip.'

Although there were men who were accused of witchcraft, the overwhelming majority of those who were indicted were female. The accused who appear in the surviving records were frequently older women, who were lacking in family support and regarded as eccentric or anti-social. These were marginalised people, even before they were denounced as witches. Those who claimed to have been bewitched were often of a higher social status than those they accused and the two parties were usually known to each other. Most witchcraft accusations took place in rural communities; there were instances in urban areas but these were more unusual.

In Medieval times, the attitude towards witches was largely benign. Wise-women, or cunning folk, who dispensed love potions along with herbal cures, claimed to find lost objects, or to tell fortunes were, for the most part, tolerated. Scholars have attempted to explain the change in outlook that resulted in an estimated 40,000 individuals, across Europe, being put to death for witchcraft in the sixteenth and seventeenth centuries. The reasons for this and the factors that prompted a wave of accusations in one particular area but not in another, are not fully understood. Why, for example, were there 473 known indictments for witchcraft in Essex but only thirty-three in Surrey? This was a period of significant social, religious and political upheaval, accompanied by a rising population, increasing poverty, civil war and epidemic disease. As Malcom Gaskill wrote, 'Our ancestors were mostly decent and intelligent people who could sink to the worst cruelty and credulity at times of intense anxiety.'

The meagre harvests of the sixteenth and seventeenth centuries meant that the poor might eat food that would otherwise be regarded as not fit for consumption. This included cereal crops, notably rye, that were infected with ergot, a toxic fungus. The resulting ergotism resulted in symptoms including paralysis, fits and hallucinations. Victims frequently complained that their skin was being pricked. These are all conditions that commonly form part of witchcraft accusations and in 1976, Linnda Caporael put forward the theory that convulsive ergotism was behind the witchcraft accusations in Salem, Massachusetts. Many scholars now disregard this as an explanation for events in Salem, but it may still have some relevance elsewhere.

Religious extremism has been blamed for what was referred to as 'the witch craze'. The power of the devil was a constant fear for adherents of the reformed Protestant church. It was thought that the devil was the only possible source of magical powers. A witch had sold her soul to the devil in return for her ability to bewitch; therefore, it was no longer possible to tolerate the activities of the cunning folk that bordered on witchcraft. In a society where the church wielded political power, heresy was only one step away from treason.

A simplistic explanation for the geographical variations in the number of accusations is that they were higher in areas where Puritan beliefs were strongly held. The tenets of Puritanism made little allowance for the dispensing of charity. Poverty was regarded as being the result of idleness and begging was thought to be a threat to social order. A way of justifying refusing a beggar charity might be to accuse them of witchcraft. It is true that persecutions might flourish against a

A Witch and a Devil making a Nail with which to make a Boy Lame, *1720. Wellcome Library, London, Wellcome Images V0025812EBL* **http://wellcomeimages.org**, *used under Creative Commons CC-BY-4.0.*

background of religious turmoil, but the picture is far more complex than equating Puritanism with increased incidences of witchcraft. Similarly, the suggestion that Parliamentarians were more likely to be persecutors and Royalists the persecuted, is an over simplification.

In the seventeenth century, women were regarded as temptresses, with sexual appetites that exceeded those of men; appetites that must be suppressed. The characteristic behaviour associated with witches was completely contrary to the acceptable conduct of a respectable, modest woman. At this time, a married woman had few rights and was expected to be subservient to her husband. Witches were often unmarried or widowed, so not under the control of men, which bred resentment. The Puritan outlook was especially condemnatory of any conduct that did not reflect the stereotypical expectation for women at this time.

It is only with the decreasing power of the church at the end of the seventeenth century, coupled with the increase in scientific thought, that more rational explanations for misfortune were sought; Renaissance philosophers equated magic with a natural science and did not regard it as having demonic connotations. Bewitching was no longer generally accepted as being possible; therefore, witches were no longer committing heresy but fraud.

Although witchcraft might include more benevolent activities, such as faith healing and herbalism, it also had its menacing side. Maleficia, actions with evil intent, included causing illness, crop failure or bad weather, ill-wishing, or, worse still, devil worship and possession. Historical witchcraft is distinct from the activities of white witches, the faith healing and herbalism of the cunning folk and far removed from Wicca, which is a modern, pagan religion.

Certain characteristics or behaviours might put an individual in danger of being accused as a witch. Swearing or blasphemy was considered common amongst witches. Acts of extreme piety were also dangerous, as witches might take communion frequently in order to appropriate the host for nefarious purposes. To be left-handed was regarded as being the mark of the devil. It is no coincidence that the Latin word for left, *sinistra*, is the root of the modern word sinister. Well into the twentieth century, school children were forced to write with their right hands. Dispensing herbal cures might be a cause for suspicion, as would having a pet, especially if the owner was seen talking to that animal, which might thus be a potential familiar. (Familiars were thought to be demons who assumed the appearance of a creature, in order to do the witch's bidding.) Having red hair could be a sign of being a witch and any skin blemishes may be the teats upon which the familiar might suck. It is not uncommon for individuals to be born with a supernumerary nipple, putting them at risk of being identified as a witch.

Witches were thought to hold sabbats, or night-time meetings, for the purposes of devil worship, excessive or abnormal sexual practices, or even cannibalism or infanticide. The sabbat was essentially a group activity and witches were thought to work in consort. Witchcraft trials involved looking for accomplices, leading to a chain of accusations and pressure on neighbours to denounce a witch, to avoid being viewed as a potential collaborator. The suggestion that witches flew at night has its origins in the cult of Diana and was largely a European phenomenon. It is interesting to note that recipes for flying ointments contain hallucinogens such as belladonna, aconite or henbane, the ingestion of which can make people believe that they are flying, hence the use of the word 'trip' for a modern drug-induced trance.

Our ancestors attempted to protect themselves from witchcraft in many ways. A witch's power was thought to work through an object, so it was inadvisable to borrow from, or lend anything to, a witch. Other measures that were seen as helpful were wearing red, or

Witches and Devils Dancing in a Circle, *1720. Wellcome Library, London, Wellcome Images V0025811ETR* **http://wellcomeimages.org**, *used under Creative Commons CC-BY-4.0.*

carrying a charm such as a phial of holy water, a stone with a hole in, or parchment containing passages from the Bible. A witch would enter a home through an opening; windows, doors and chimneys therefore needed protection. This might be done by burying a bellamine, or witch bottle, under the lintel, or threshold, or in the chimney. These stoneware bottles were often filled with pins, hair, or urine. Planting a bay tree by the cottage door was thought to, quite literally, keep the witches at bay; rue was another herb that might have protective powers.

Victims of bewitchment could seek an antidote. Fire was regarded as purifying, so the bewitched item might be burned. Burning something belonging to a suspected witch was thought to make her appear, then she could be asked to remove her curse. Witchfinders acted in a similar way to modern bailiffs; they attempted to bring witches to trial in return for monetary rewards. The most notorious were Matthew Hopkins, the self-styled Witchfinder General and his associate, John Sterne. They were responsible for the high number of convictions in Essex and surrounding counties during the 1640s.

The first English witchcraft legislation was passed in the mid-sixteenth century. A short-lived, rarely invoked, statute of the 1540s was replaced in 1563, by an 'Acte Againste Conjuracons, Inchantments and Witchcraftes'. This set out a range of offences that might be considered to be witchcraft, including causing injury, or searching for treasure. A first offence would lead to a one-year prison sentence but like many offences at this time, it would be accompanied by an act of public penance or humiliation. The offender was required to:

> once in every Quarter of the said Yere, shall in some Market towne, upon the Market Daye or at such tyme as any Fayer shal bee kepte there, stande openly upon the Pillorie by the Space of Syxe Houres, and there shall openly confesse his or her Erroure and Offence.

A second offence would result in life imprisonment. Causing death by witchcraft, or invoking evil spirits, were both punishable by death. In Europe, the upsurge in witchcraft accusations was known as 'The Burning Time' but in England and Wales witches were not put to death by burning, instead they were hanged.

James I had an equivocal relationship with witchcraft. He denounced witches in his 1597 publication *Daemonologie* and his statute of 1604 established the death penalty for a second conviction of witchcraft and for a first offence leading to harm. Crucially, this act also punished 'aydes, abettors and councellors', something that made association with known witches all the more dangerous. In 1618, a manual for Justices of the Peace stressed the importance of investigating the character and family of all those accused of crimes. This had a particular significance in trials for witchcraft, as they were conducted slightly differently from cases involving other crimes. Normally, minors and the spouses of the accused could not give evidence, but this was not the case for witchcraft. In addition, what were described as 'half proofes' were allowed and a confession was regarded as irrefutable proof. The 1604 act was repealed in 1736, by which time few people believed that one individual could bewitch another.

Contrary to popular opinion, witches were not ducked. Ducking was for scolds or gossips. Instead, witches would be swum. This was a remnant of trial by ordeal and was not supposed to be used, although the witchfinder Stearne claimed that the women requested it. The left thumb was tied to the right big toe and the right thumb to the left big toe. A rope would be put round the accused's waist and they would be thrown into a pond or river. Those who floated were considered guilty. Sinking was an indicator of innocence but might well have resulted in drowning the individual on trial.

Once apprehended, an accused witch would be searched for the devil's marks. Pricking for a witch involved inserting a needle into the marks. If they bled, the woman was innocent but if they did not, this was 'unnatural' and added to the evidence that she was a witch. In fact, the implement used to prick the witch was often designed so that the needle retracted into the handle, meaning that the skin was not broken.

Unlike crimes such as burglary or assault, it was impossible to witness the act of witchcraft, only the alleged effects of it. In cases of witchcraft, referral to the courts was based on 'common fame', in other words, rumour. It was therefore ideal if a witch could be 'persuaded' to confess. The accused would be sleep-deprived and made to walk through the night. Watchers would be observing to see if a familiar visited the witch. The most damning evidence against a witch was her own confession, or the accusation of another witch.

It was acceptable to use physical means to try to extract a confession; any confession given under duress was supposed to be ratified later. Although, in theory, the drawing of blood was not allowed, tortures involving crushing were seen as acceptable. Finger crushers or thumb screws, known as pilliwinks, might be used. Nails were ripped out and the breasts or genitals removed. Bootikins were leg braces that could be tightened, and the strappado involved tying the victim's arms behind their back and suspending them by the wrists, thereby dislocating

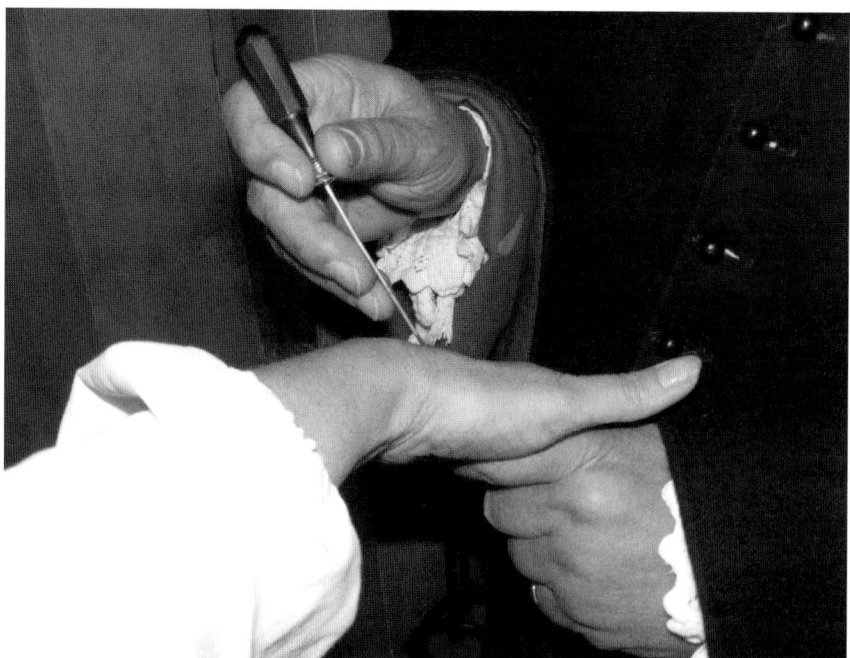

Pricking for a Witch © *Janet Few.*

their shoulders. Thrawing comprised twisting ropes round the head. The pear of anguish was particularly gruesome. It was a pear-shaped metal implement that could be inserted into an orifice before being expanded and forcibly withdrawn. It is clear that many of these tortures would have involved drawing blood.

In an attempt to get charges dropped, the accused might go through a process known as purgation. Not only did they need to swear their innocence but they had to persuade others to support them, testifying as to their good character. The nature of witchcraft cases meant that the accused were often ostracised by their neighbours, making this difficult. People would be very reluctant to show support for a witch, as it might lead to them being viewed as an accomplice.

In England, witchcraft was essentially a secular crime, associated with bewitching rather than heresy. Witches might, however, have been tried in the ecclesiastical or secular courts and court records are one of the first places to seek evidence of witchcraft trials. Following the statute of 1604, cases of witchcraft were more likely to be dealt with in a secular court. Occasionally, an individual appears in both the civil and ecclesiastical records but it is not always clear if they were tried for the same offence twice, or if they had been accused on more than one occasion. The Quarter Sessions Courts did not have the power to try witches but examinations often began there, before being referred to the assizes. This means that gaol records and recognisances for the appearance of the accused, the accusers and witnesses can be found in county record offices. The records that can be used to trace all criminals, described in Chapter 2, can also be used to look for references to those accused of witchcraft.

Broadsheets were often printed, providing salacious and frequently inaccurate, accounts of accusations and witchcraft trials. Other evidence might include diaries, letters, biographies or sermons. The records resulting from ecclesiastical visitations are held in diocesan record offices, usually combined with the county archives. Names are rarely given but for example, Bishop's Visitations of 1628 asked, 'Have you any in your parish, which have used any enchantments, sorceries, witchcrafts, or incantations?' Pardons for witchcraft might be found in State Papers at The National Archives. Many accused witches, who were often elderly and victims of torture, died in prison whilst awaiting trial. This could result in a coroner's inquest that may survive.

In an era of political and social turmoil, anxiety is paramount as people feel vulnerable. Psychologically, it is easier to cope with fear or threat if the perception is that the source of that threat comes from an outsider, thus the tendency to try to blame misfortune on the marginalised, through the conduit of witchcraft. Historically, anyone who was accused of witchcraft was despised. Now, sympathy lies with the accused and researchers are perhaps more uncomfortable if they discover family members amongst the accusers.

The Story of Susanna Edwards

Susanna was baptised in 1612 in Bideford, Devon, the illegitimate daughter of Rachel Winslade. Rachel descended from an armigerous local family that had suffered for their Catholicism and their involvement in the Prayer Book Rebellion of 1549. Rachel had a second illegitimate daughter in 1620. Unlike many accused witches, Susanna was married; her children and grandchildren were living locally at the time of her accusation. There is of course no way of knowing if her family had disassociated themselves from her.

Susanna had married David or Davy Edwards, in Bideford, in 1639. It is possible that her husband had come from Wales; he does not appear to have been local. There was a great deal of movement between the North Devon port of Bideford across the Bristol Channel to South Wales at this time. Six children were baptised in Bideford before Davy's death in 1662. The sources for what happened to Susanna are fragmentary and, in some cases, contradictory. One broadsheet does not even give the correct names for those who were accused with Susanna, bringing the reliability of the remainder of the account into question. It appears that events unfolded as follows.

In the summer of 1680, Susanna visited Dorcas Coleman, the wife of a mariner, possibly to ask for charity. Dorcas was subsequently taken ill, complaining of prickings in her arms, stomach and heart. When Dorcas claimed to see Susanna in her chamber, her husband John attempted to go after Susanna but his wife's collapse prevented him. The doctor was summoned. Unable to explain Dorcas's apparent paralysis, Doctor Beare claimed that she had been bewitched. This seems to have been a convenient loophole for a doctor who was incapable of providing a satisfactory diagnosis.

On 1 July 1682, Temperance Lloyd was arrested for witchcraft in Bideford. This was the beginning of a summer of accusations in the town. Temperance was notorious, having been acquitted of witchcraft on two previous occasions. Grace Barnes, wife of John Barnes, a yeoman, had been afflicted for many years but had not suspected witchcraft until, early in 1681, a physician told her that she was bewitched. This may have been the same doctor who had attended Dorcas Coleman. Grace began to suspect Susanna because of her unsolicited visits to the house. In July 1682, Grace's condition worsened and at that moment, found a woman named Mary Trembles passing the door. It is likely that Mary was taking food to be baked in one of the town's communal ovens, as many homes at this time did not have facilities for cooking, apart from an open fire. Mary dropped the pot she was carrying and this was seen by Grace as a ruse, whereby Mary could ill-wish her. Mary Trembles was duly arrested, along with Susanna Edwards.

Susanna and Mary were taken to the town lock-up, where members of the community came to gawp and to question the two women. Allegedly, Susanna admitted to being a witch but John Dunning, to whom she supposedly made this confession, was never called as a witness. It was hearsay evidence from one Joan Jones, who claimed to have overheard the conversation between Dunning and Susanna, that was then related to the justices in Bideford Guildhall. During the hearing, Anthony Jones, Joan's husband, asserted that Susanna was, at that moment, 'twinkling' her hands and bewitching someone. Mr Jones went to help the constables fetch Grace Barnes, in order that she could present her evidence. On returning to the court room, Anthony had some form of fit and claimed that this was Susanna's work. John Barnes, Grace's husband, accused Mary of causing his wife's affliction by witchcraft. Mary, when questioned, laid the blame for her initiation into witchcraft firmly at Susanna's door.

Local blacksmith, William Edwards, maintained that he had overheard Susanna confessing to having carnal knowledge with the devil and admitting to invisibly entering the Barnes home with Mary Trembles. When Susanna was questioned, she confessed to the charges, including admitting to pricking and tormenting Dorcas Coleman. Did she really believe herself to be responsible for these women's afflictions? Was she so worn down by events that she was willing to agree to anything? Both Susanna and Mary were taken back to the lock-up where their bodies were searched for any skin blemishes that might be teats through which they suckled the devil. As these marks were thought likely to be hidden in the genitalia, this would have been a humiliating and horrific experience.

Susanna and Mary were transferred to the county town of Exeter, some 40 miles away, to await trial at the next sitting of the assize court, where Temperance Lloyd was also to be tried. Two days later, two other Bideford women were also accused of witchcraft. The case against one, Mary Beare, or Beard, did not progress. Elizabeth Caddy joined Susanna and Mary in Exeter but her case was dismissed for lack of evidence. It is interesting to note that both Mary Beare and Elizabeth were of a higher social standing than Susanna and Mary Trembles.

These accusations in Bideford were atypical in some ways. The peak of accusations had passed by this time. Most accusations took place in poverty-stricken, rural areas, yet the time of Susanna's accusation coincided with the start of forty years of economic prominence for the port of Bideford. The town was home to many wealthy merchants, most of whom were not locally born. There was, however, a strong tradition of non-conformity and many were adherents of the Independent Chapel; this almost certainly contributed to the attitudes that held sway in the town. Many accusations did take place in areas where puritanical views predominated. Bideford's revised charter, granted in 1610, extended the size and role of the council, empowering it to conduct enquiries 'of all and every murders, felonies, witchcrafts, incantations, sorceries, art and magic'.

The harvests of 1682 were particularly unproductive and it was a time of food shortages. The divide between the poor of Bideford and the prosperous merchant class in the town was increasingly evident. Mary Trembles claimed that she and Susanna had gone to the Barnes's house begging for food and when that was refused, they asked for tobacco instead, which was no more successful.

As Mary Trembles was also accused of bewitching Grace Barnes and two people could not be severally tried for the same crime, the final indictment against Susanna related solely to the bewitching of Dorcas Coleman. Despite Susanna's earlier 'confession', at the trial she and her two co-accused, pleaded not guilty.

The evidence against Susanna came largely from Joan Jones and William Edwards, both of whom were relying on hearsay. Joan Jones's fanciful account gave details of Susanna's alleged association with the devil, which, she said, took place in Parsonage Close. Jones also maintained that Susanna had admitted to bewitching Dorcas Coleman, a woman who, before her marriage, had been one of the accusers at an earlier trial of Temperance Lloyd. At the last minute, Dorcas Coleman, her husband John, and Thomas Bremmicombe, claimed to have remembered additional incidents. This included Dorcas's claim that Susanna was responsible for an illness she had suffered two years earlier. Whilst Susannah was in Exeter prison, she was questioned by a clergyman, Mr Hann, who attested that the devil had also been present during his visit to the gaol.

The statement of Mary Trembles was particularly damning. She said that Susanna had initiated her into witchcraft three years earlier, promising that she, Mary, should not want for money, meat, drink or clothes if she would lie with the devil. In her turn, Susanna blamed Temperance Lloyd and the gossip in the town was of the opinion that Temperance was the ringleader.

Sir Francis North, the Lord Chief Justice, was due to preside over the trial but was taken ill at the last minute. This was unfortunate, as North had a very enlightened outlook and was questioning the existence of witchcraft. In North's absence, the trial was conducted by Judge Thomas

Raymond, who had grown up in East Anglia at the height of the Essex witchcraft accusations; this must surely have coloured his outlook. Had North been presiding, the outcome might have been different. Public opinion was, however, vociferous and overwhelmingly condemnatory; had the women been freed, it was likely that there would have been an outcry. The fear of a popular uprising almost certainly played its part in the final verdict.

The three women were taken back to Exeter gaol where they waited for the sentence to be carried out. The records suggest that they were the last three women to be executed for witchcraft in England. This took place on 25 August 1682, in front of a huge crowd. Susanna was again questioned by Reverend Hann. She denied that she was a witch. After Hann led the prayers, Susanna asked that the fortieth psalm should be sung. The first of the three to mount the scaffold was Susanna. Her final words were, 'The Lord Jesus speed me; though my sins be red as scarlet the Lord Jesus can make me white as snow.'

A more detailed account of Susanna's story and the events and local attitudes that led to her accusation, can be found in the author's fictionalised account 'Sins as Red as Scarlet'.

Chapter 11

OTHER MARGINALISED GROUPS

There are many other groups who were victims of prejudice in the past. This chapter discusses those who were marginalised because of their religious beliefs or their sexuality, and also looks at those who were stigmatised because they were conscientious objectors or deserters in times of conflict.

Religious Belief

It may be unexpected to find non-conformists included in a book about marginalised ancestors but historically, followers of certain religious groups were not accepted by their contemporaries who adhered to other faiths. Those whose way of worship was different to whatever brand of religion prevailed at the time risked being ostracised, discriminated against and at times, actively persecuted. As long ago as the twelfth century, there were anti-Semitic riots in various cities in eastern England. In the wake of the religious turbulence of the sixteenth century and the Reformation, intolerance of dissent, on both sides of the religious spectrum, reached a peak. In the seventeenth century, measures were enacted against both Protestant non-conformists and Catholics. The Toleration Act of 1689 changed the official policy towards those outwith the Church of England but prejudices remained.

Quakers, Methodists and many other 'ists' were regarded as being different and caused the establishment concern; religious dissent was equated, in the minds of many, with political subversion. In *The Gentleman's Magazine* of 1744, the vicar of St Ives in Cornwall described Methodists as 'the new sect ... enemies of the Church, Jacobites, Papists and what not'. This level of misunderstanding is indicative of the prejudices of the time. The fear that non-conformists were a threat to social order was fuelled by the tendency for evangelical sects to preach

A Catalogue of the several Sects and Opinions in England and other Nations, *Broadsheet 1647, British Museum. Image in the public domain.*

in public, giving free rein to hecklers. These groups of non-conformists also targeted the very events and institutions that had previously held communities together, by holding open-air services at the village fete, on sports days, or where people gathered to attend market.

An extract from the biography of Quaker Thomas Ellwood describes an incident that took place in 1666:

> At a Quaker Meeting at the Bull and Mouth, by Aldersgate, when on a sudden, a party of soldiers (of the trained bands of the city) rushed in with noise and clamour, being led by one who was called Major Rosewell, an apothecary, (if I remember not) and at that time came under the ill name of a Papist. As soon as he was come within the room, having a file or two of musketeers at his heels, he commanded his men to present their muskets to us, which they did with intent, I suppose, to strike terror into the people.

This is only Ellwood's side of the story, but to confront a group of worshippers, renowned for their peaceful tendencies, with a group of armed men, is illustrative of the reaction to non-conformity at the time.

Religion in general and non-conformity in particular, had implications for mental health. Belonging to a religious community can be very comforting and give members a sense of belonging. In the past, religion went beyond being an opportunity for worship. An individual's employer and landlord would probably be part of the same denomination. One's social life revolved round the church or chapel.

Add to this the 'hellfire and damnation' nature of many non-conformist sermons and a situation was created whereby those who moved outside the religious community, or felt they had transgressed in some way, believed that they had forfeited everything, including their soul. As we saw in Chapters 7 and 8, many case books for patients in asylums cite some form of 'religious mania' as a reason for incarceration.

The lives of all our ancestors, non-conformist or not, were shaped by the factionalism that arose from the rise of non-conformity and also by the demographic dislocations that resulted from the numerous emigrations, that were a feature of belonging to some religious groups. The communities created by the non-conformist congregations provided security and a sense of belonging for many followers. Yet, non-conformity was seen, by those outside its embrace, as being responsible for dividing communities and was associated with disloyalty and insurgency. Whilst religious groups formed unified communities of their own, at the same time they served to fragment the wider geographical community in which they were found and many villages experienced damaging church–chapel divides. Michael Snape, in his book *Anti-Methodism in Eighteenth-Century England* wrote that, those within the established church 'were concerned to protect their Church, their king, their families, their livelihoods and the integrity of their communities'. One way of achieving this was through the marginalisation of non-conformity and its adherents.

In 1676, Bishop Henry Compton required all incumbents in England and Wales to list the numbers of conformists (Anglicans), papists (Catholics) and non-conformists, in their parish. The resulting statistics are arranged by Anglican parish and give an impression of levels of non-conformity in the area. The surviving returns are for the Midlands, Wales and the South of England. There are copies at the William Salt Library, Staffordshire, **www.staffordshire.gov.uk/leisure/archives/williamsalt/home.aspx** and The Bodleian Library, Oxford **www.bodleian.ox.ac.uk**. A transcription of the returns has been edited by Annie Whiteman and published by Oxford University Press.

The Ecclesiastical Census of 1851 gives an overview of what options for worship were available in a particular area. At this time, there were 22,900 places of worship in England and Wales, 60 per cent of which were not part of the established Church of England. The original Ecclesiastical Census returns are in class HO129 at The National Archives. The returns, arranged by Anglican parish, can be downloaded from The National Archives website **http://discovery.nationalarchives.gov.uk/browse/r/h/C8993**.

The Non-Parochial Registers Act of 1840 required that all non-conformist registers should be surrendered to the Registrar General. These are now at The National Archives. Many non-conformist records of baptisms, marriages and burials, covering Methodists, Wesleyans, Baptists, Independents, Protestant Dissenters, Congregationalist, Presbyterians, Unitarians and Quakers (Society of Friends), are now available online at the subscription website The Genealogist; some are also available on other websites.

Each denomination has its own records and resources; there are suggestions for further reading at the end of this book that will help with researching particular religious groups. The National Archives also has several useful research guides on the subject.

Sexuality

Intolerance, and the fact that male homosexuality was a criminal offence in Britain until 1967, makes it difficult to identify relatives who belonged to sections of what we now call the LGBTQ+ community. Societal pressures meant that many would have been living an outwardly heterosexual lifestyle, or would have remained celibate. There may be family stories, letters, or diaries suggesting that individuals were in a gay relationship, but in the nineteenth and early twentieth centuries, people of the same sex might write to each other in quite passionate terms, without the friendship being sexual.

Evidence of both male and female same-sex relationships can occasionally be found in reports of divorce cases. Census returns might disguise partners as lodgers. If a couple were living together over many years, it could be that their connection went beyond that of landlord or landlady and lodger. In 1795, gardener Henry Poole of Reading wrote his will, in which he referred to his male 'friend and intimate acquaintance', to whom he left a ring 'in memory of me'. It is subtle suggestions such as these that might imply that an individual was gay. An individual's appearance, or failure to marry, might be also be indicative, but we should not categorically impose a sexuality on a relative using ambiguous evidence; this includes assuming that marriage and parenthood is proof of unwavering heterosexuality. What is important is acknowledging and recording known incidences of same-sex relationships within our families, in the same way as we might any other union and ensuring that people appear in the family records with their preferred gender. Sadly, genealogical software does not always facilitate this.

This topic needs to be considered within the context of the times. Most of the words that are now used to describe people who are in same-sex relationships are comparatively new, or have been repurposed. The word homosexual was not coined until 1868; 'gay' had a different meaning in the 1960s, let alone the 1860s. In the past, other terms, such as catamite, Molly or Mary Ann, all with derogatory overtones, would have been used.

For many of our ancestors, their only knowledge of non-heterosexual relationships would be brief Biblical references. Our relatives who found that they were not attracted to the opposite sex might remain single or conform to expectations and marry. Many would be too frightened of legal or societal repercussions to pursue a relationship with someone of the same sex. They might not be aware of anyone who was not heterosexual, or even realise that there was another option, albeit, in the case of men, one that would be illegal. The combined forces of public opinion and religious doctrine made embarking on a same-sex relationship extremely difficult; something that many would shy away from, regardless of their preferences. It was considered normal and acceptable for gay men to be medically treated for what were deemed to be 'unnatural urges', using electroconvulsive therapy, aversion therapy, or lobotomy. In Britain, this situation persisted into the second half of the twentieth century and is indicative of the way that gay people were generally regarded.

This is not to suggest that gay relationships did not occur at all levels of society. Sadly, the majority of the unequivocal evidence is available only because homosexuality was illegal. The *Yorkshire Gazette* of 6 December 1845, reported that Joseph Carter, aged 55, was accused of feloniously assaulting Henry Brown and committing the 'abominable' crime of sodomy. The inclusion of the adjective is symptomatic of the attitudes of the time; 'abominable' was not used to describe other offences, such as burglaries. From Scotland's Court and Criminal Database **www.scottishindexes.com/ScotlandsCriminalDatabase.aspx**, we learn that on 29 December 1845 Ralph Dodds and William Simpson confessed to attempted sodomy in Campbell's Close, Cowgate, Edinburgh and were sentenced to transportation for ten years. It is references such as these that may be the only evidence of a relative's sexuality.

It is more difficult to find evidence of lesbian relationships, largely because they were not against the law. There is a suggestion that Queen Victoria initially refused to give her assent to the Criminal Law Amendment Act, which criminalised gross indecency between men. Allegedly, she rejected the first draft because it included the outlawing of relationships between women, which she did not believe existed. Although this is a myth, the lack of awareness of lesbianism, in society as a whole, should not be overlooked.

Amongst the high-profile, usually wealthy, women, such as Radclyffe Hall, who liked to wear clothes traditionally reserved for men, there are documented instances of women across the social scale dressing as men. The burial register of Etherly, Durham, contains the following entry in 1868, 'Joseph Josiah Charles Stephenson. A woman, name unknown, who had lived as and passed for a man under the name stated, thought to be about 80 years old.' In the mid-eighteenth century, Hannah Snell, who had been married and had borne a child, assumed a male identity and fought in the Royal Marines. These individuals fall within the LGBTQ+ sphere and their behaviour might well be indicative of their preferred sexual partners. For some, however, the primary motivating force behind living as a man might be a desire to experience a role that was otherwise denied to them by society.

Hannah Snell, *John Faber. Image in the public domain, accessed via Wikimedia Commons.*

As mentioned above, the criminalisation of homosexuality means that gay family members might appear in court records or in newspaper accounts of trials. The Buggery Act was on the statute books from 1533 to 1828. This went beyond making male same-sex relationships illegal, as it also encompassed male–female sodomy and bestiality. The Act was replaced by The Offences against the Person Act, which retained the death penalty for acts of male homosexuality. An Act of 1861 replaced the death penalty with a prison sentence, with hard labour, for a minimum of ten years. Gross indecency was outlawed by the Criminal Law Amendment Act in 1885. There was an attempt, in 1921, to criminalise lesbian relationships but this failed. It was feared that the passing of the act would draw attention to the possibility of female same-sex relationships, thus making them more prevalent.

Anyone wishing to explore this topic further, should read Gill Rossini's *Same-sex Love 1700–1957: A History and Research Guide* and there is further suggested reading at the end of this book.

Conscientious Objection and Desertion

Patriotism was a very strongly held principle and the willingness and ability to take up arms for one's country in times of war was regarded as a manifestation of this. Anyone whose conscience precluded armed combat, or who deserted, was branded a coward and both they and, by association, their families, were stigmatised.

In Britain, the Military Service Act introduced conscription in early 1916, making able-bodied, single men and childless widowers, aged 19 to 40, liable for military service; clergymen, teachers, doctors and those working in essential industries were exempt. In the summer of 1916, this was extended to include 18-year-olds, married men and widowers with children. The upper age limit was increased to 51 in April 1918. As a result of the efforts of the No-Conscription Fellowship, a conscience clause was included in the act and 16,000 men refused to serve on religious, political or moral grounds. They then faced the rigors of a military tribunal. Many appeals for exemption on the ground of conscientious objection were turned down and the objector would then be conscripted into the army.

In March 1916, the Non-combatant Corps was formed and 10,000 served in this way, rather than taking up arms. Some joined the Friends' Ambulance Unit, which included some non-Quakers amongst its personnel. Record cards for men serving with the Friends' Ambulance Unit, most of which include photographs, are available online at **http://fau.quaker.org.uk/search-view**. George Harold Braund, the son of a Yorkshire Anglican rector but whose mother's family had Quaker connections, was granted absolute exemption on the grounds of conscientious objection and joined the unit in 1915. His record card provides his date of birth, address, next of kin and details of his vaccinations. It also reveals that George was an undergraduate at Queen's College, Cambridge and spoke a little French. He served in France as an orderly for three years.

In July 1916, the Home Office Scheme gave conscientious objectors the opportunity to work in labour camps as an alternative to prison. Some of the 'alternativists' who became part of this scheme were moved to Dartmoor Prison, where they were set to work building dry-stone walls, that were then demolished and rebuilt; others were tasked with digging ditches. The journal of the prison's medical officer survives and may refer to named men. About 6,000 men, known as absolutists, refused to obey Home Office orders, as they were not willing to do anything to support the war effort and were therefore imprisoned.

National Service, sometimes then called War Service, was reintroduced in 1939. By 1942, all men aged 18 to 51 and all unmarried women and childless widows, aged 20 to 30, were liable to be called up. National Service continued in peacetime, with 17- to 20-year-old men being expected to serve for eighteen months and then remain on the reserve list for a further four years; certain essential occupations were exempted. The last conscripts were discharged in 1963.

In the Second World War, 60,000 men and 1,000 women registered as conscientious objectors. By 1939, attitudes towards armed conflict, shaped by the experience of the First World War, had shifted and although there was still discrimination, hostility towards those who embraced anti-war sentiments was, for the most part, less extreme. The Military Training Act came into force in May 1939, requiring all men aged 20 and 21 to register at the Labour Exchange, to undergo a medical and then embark on six months' military training. This Act acknowledged the option of conscientious objection, in what was known as a conscience clause. Once war was declared, conscription was immediately extended to all men aged 18 to 41.

Anyone wishing to refuse military service had to provide a written statement of their reasons, substantiated by witness statements or references. They would then appear before a tribunal, who would consider their case. The approach to conscientious objection was slightly different during the Second World War, when tribunals were the responsibility of the Ministry of Labour. There were sixteen tribunals overseeing cases in different parts of Britain and two appeals tribunals, one in London and one in Edinburgh. The five people who made up the panel that assessed the sincerity of the applicant's beliefs, were civilians, rather than military personnel.

Those granted unconditional exemption were placed on the Register of Conscientious Objectors. Conditional exemption meant that the objector either had to agree to serve in a non-combatant role within the military – ambulance driving or firefighting for example – or they had to undertake work or training, as specified by Ministry of Labour, before they could be entered on the register.

Some tribunals were more sympathetic than others and the personality of the presiding judge impacted on this. The North Midlands tribunal granted very few unconditional exemptions and nearly a third of those who appeared before them were placed on the military register. By comparison, in the South West only 10 per cent had their appeal for some kind of exemption refused.

Very few records of conscientious objectors survive. The National Archives has a research guide that might be useful **www.nationalarchives.gov.uk/help-with-your-research/research-guides/conscientious-objectors/**. There may be reports of tribunals in newspapers, although these were often underreported, as they were seen to be damaging to morale. During the Second World War, Scottish newspapers seemed to report the outcomes of tribunals more fully than English publications, including naming objectors. On 2 February 1917, the *Western Chronicle* reported:

> Thomas Bailey, a milk vendor and well-known conscientious objector to military service, appeared to an adjourned charge

at Exeter for non-compliance with the [Military Service] Act. The magistrates told him he would be handed over to the military. The defendant complained that he had not been dealt with fairly and declared that he would never be a soldier.

THE TRIBUNAL

No. 155   THURSDAY, MAY 1, 1919   One Penny

MAY-DAY, 1919.

To our comrades fighting against militarism and conscription here and abroad,
To our friends in prison,
To all those struggling for freedom and peace in every part of the world,
To the men and women of all countries,
   —May-Day Greetings from the No Conscription Fellowship.
            Away with Conscription !
            Away with Militarism !

May 1st, 1919.   Hail to the International Friendship of Free Peoples !

STILL UNDAUNTED.

Up to date 665 men have been released from their prison cells, and the N.C.F. headquarters are being inundated with letters from these brave comrades of ours. The letters are a revelation in every way. Prison has not crushed, nor adversity dulled, the spirit of those who have come out. One and all are anxious to be up and doing. Nearly all of them thank those who have carried on the work of the organisation, as if anyone deserved thanks but themselves. The work of those outside was only rendered possible by their endurance. Now they are beginning to come back and their first thought is of the boys they left behind. Their letters should be an inspiration to us all. Below are a few extracts taken almost at random from a huge pile of correspondence.

J. CROMPTON : " It has been a great fight, and I feel now I can hold up my head before the world and still work earnestly for Liberty and Freedom, and still battle against Militarism."

JAMES SLAVEN : " On leaving prison five of us were conscripted by the N.C.F. and sentenced to a month's holiday, but we are wishing to be back at propaganda to do our bit in gaining the speedy release of those whom we were forced to leave behind."

J. McINNIMIE : " I should like to know what ideas prevail at Headquarters with reference to the future, and if I can help even in a small way in any propaganda work while I am recuperating . . . I feel as if I am not wholly free as long as one C.O. is left in prison. "

GEORGE H. PEET : " If I can do anything to advance our cause, especially anything on behalf of our comrades still in prison, please let me know."

ROBERT STEWART : " I am a bit shaky after two-and-a-half years in the insanitorium, so you will excuse short scrawl. A long and a strong pull now and downs goes conscription. Release, resist and repeal must be our immediate slogan.

" Release, Resist, Repeal ! " 300 comrades are still in prison.—Release ! Militarism is still the enemy—Resist ! Conscription is still on the statute book.—Repeal ! "

The undaunted example of those who have endured for freedom's sake must be an inspiration to us all. Meetings must be organised. Branches must be revived. The circulation of the *Tribunal* must go up by leaps and bounds. Each in his or her own way must give the best that is in them to the common cause. The first stage in the battle is drawing to an end. Our members have shown beyond contradiction their ability to resist. Now, far and wide, those who have resisted must carry a message to all the people telling them of the great hope that has been born into the world. The hope that war can end and will end when the objectors are not few but many.

" Then, comrades, come rally,
The last fight let us face,
The L'Internationale
Unites the human race."

C.Os STILL GOING TO PRISON.

More than five months after the armistice, conscientious objectors are still being court-martialled and committed to imprisonment. One of the latest cases is that of E. J. Llewellyn, a Welshman, who was first court-martialled on November 1st, 1918, and taken to Wormwood Scrubbs. On appeal, the sentence was quashed and Llewellyn was removed to Cardiff Barracks. He has now been re-courtmartialled, sentenced to one year's hard labour and confined in Cardiff Prison.

The Tribunal *1919. Image in the public domain.*

The records of the appeal tribunals for Middlesex survive in MH47 at The National Archives and can be downloaded via **www.nationalarchives.gov.uk**. These records include details for John London, of Wood Green, a cinematograph operator. He requested absolute exemption on the grounds that military service would cause serious hardship owing to his domestic position; this was a valid basis for possible exemption under the terms of the Military Service Act. He stated that his wife had consumption and was 'generally nervous'. He had six children, the oldest of whom was 12. The local tribunal had decided that no serious hardship would ensue if John was conscripted. As a result of the appeal, John was initially granted a temporary exemption of fourteen days 'to make arrangements' but then his subsequent appeal was dismissed. National Records of Scotland hold some tribunal records for Lothian and Peebles in class HH30. Lists of appeals relating to the period 1939–1962 are held in class LAB45 at The National Archives; the catalogue entry begins 'Most of the National Service documents have been destroyed and only these few samples from the Midland region have survived.'

During the First World War, over 3,000 men serving with the British and Commonwealth forces were sentenced to death for desertion and one in ten of these men faced the firing squad; some were as young as 16. In 2006, the British government officially pardoned all 306 men who had been put to death in this way. The regulations governing the conduct of courts martial were changed for the duration of the hostilities, allowing them to be carried out by three officers presiding over a field general court martial. These took place within twenty-four hours and there was no right to appeal. Many of these servicemen would have been suffering from what was to be called shell-shock and is now known as PTSD; they were ill, not cowards. Trying to trace a deserter's story can be difficult, as they might well have changed their name to try to avoid capture.

The Police Gazette regularly published the names of deserters and those for 1914–1919 are available on Findmypast. The entries give regiment, a physical description, age, home parish and details of peacetime occupation. For example, Reginald Moore of the 1st Shropshire Light Infantry appears in the issue for 11 August 1914. He absconded on 25 July 1914 at Netheravon, Wiltshire. There were many other soldiers deserting in July 1914, perhaps a consequence of anticipating that war would be declared. The entry states that Reginald was from Ludlow, Shropshire, aged 20¾, was 5ft 5½in tall, with a sallow complexion, brown hair and grey eyes. He had a scar on the right side of his chin. Reginald had been a waggoner before he enlisted on 7 June 1912 at Shrewsbury.

Service records will also reveal if a relative deserted, or was absent without leave. There may be clues in other records. On the 1921 census form, Alice Lemon wrote 'husband deserter if could be found could you let the ploice [sic] know, Charles John Lemon'.

The Story of William Wilcox

William was born on 17 August 1860 at Natcott Lane, in Hartland, Devon; he was the sixth of seven children of Richard and Ann Wilcox née Harris; William's mother died in childbirth, when he was 6. Hartland, on the north coast of Devon, is predominantly rural. By the age of 11, William was working as a general servant on Hescott Farm.

In February 1877, when William was 16½, he travelled to Cardiff, where he enlisted into the 2nd battalion of the 24th Foot, thereby committing himself to six years' army service, followed by six years in the army reserve. He claimed that he was 18 years and 3 months old. William was described as being 5ft 7½in tall, with a sallow complexion, hazel eyes and dark hair; he was unable to sign his name. Unusually, he was listed as a Roman Catholic. At no other point in his life is there any indication that he was Catholic. Although there were few Catholics in north Devon at this time, there was a Catholic church in Hartland.

William spent some time in Dover and Chatham in Kent. In February 1878, he sailed, with his unit, for the Cape of Good Hope, to take part in the Zulu wars, where both the 1st and 2nd Battalions of the 24th Regiment of Foot served. William's army service record states that he contracted pneumonia in early February 1878, perhaps on the journey. In January 1879, some of William's comrades were involved in the Battle of Isandlwana, from which only two survived. Meanwhile, William himself, along with most of the 2nd Battalion, was at nearby Rorke's Drift, where they had been instructed to guard the hospital and supply depot.

News came that there was trouble at Isandlwana and that a Zulu force was heading for Rorke's Drift. Defences were hastily constructed using biscuit boxes and sacks of animal feed. The auxiliary contingent of Natal Native Horse withdrew, leaving only 153 men to protect Rorke's Drift, some of whom were seriously ill hospital patients. The Zulu force was estimated to be 3,000–4,000. The battle involved hand-to-hand fighting within the hospital, which was set on fire. The following day, reinforcements arrived and the Zulus retreated. The fact that a record eleven Victoria Crosses were awarded to men who fought at Rorke's Drift, gives an indication of the severity of the battle.

It was not, however, this traumatic encounter that led William to desert. His battalion remained at Rorke's Drift, living under very challenging conditions. For three months, there were no tents available, so the men were forced to sleep on the ground, and thirty men died. William's army statement of service reveals that he deserted on 28 October 1879; he was still only 18 years old. William rejoined the unit on 1 November; it is not clear if this was voluntarily, or if he was captured. He was tried and imprisoned for desertion and theft, forfeiting all his good conduct pay. William remained in prison until September 1881, so, in the 1881 census, he can be found amongst the prisoners at Forton Military Prison in Gosport, Hampshire where he was serving a sentence of 672 days with hard labour. On release, he was transferred to the 1st Battalion and served with them until February 1889.

On discharge, William returned to his native Hartland and worked as a steam-engine driver. He married Lily Vanstone in 1891 and the couple had one daughter. Apart from one incident, William avoided falling foul of the authorities for the rest of his life. In 1905, when he was driving his steam-engine down a narrow lane in Hartland, he was fined £1 for not sending a man in front to warn approaching vehicles. Providing advance warning was deemed necessary, so that other traffic would not have to turn back when meeting his steam-engine coming in the other direction.

William died on 29 May 1925 aged 64 and was buried in an unmarked grave in Dolton churchyard, Devon. In 2011, a headstone was erected in his memory by the great-grandson of one of William's comrades.

REFERENCES AND FURTHER READING

A Few Forgotten Women **https://afewforgottenwomen.wixsite.com/affw**
Carve her Name **https://carvehername.org.uk/about-us/**
Friends of Horton Cemetery **https://hortoncemetery.org/**
Hidden Lives Revealed: a virtual archive of children in care **www.hiddenlives.org.uk**
Project Infant commemorating the lives of those in Irish mother and baby homes **https://projectinfant.ie/**

Chapter 1: Poverty
Further Reading
Bagley, John J. & Bagley, Alexander John, *The English Poor Law* (Macmillan 1968)
Burlison, Robert, *Tracing your Pauper Ancestors: a guide for family historians* (Pen and Sword 2009)
Cole, Anne, *An Introduction to Poor Law Documents before 1834* (FFHS 2nd edition 2000)
Fowler, Simon, *Workhouse: The People, The Places, The Life Behind Doors* (Pen and Sword 2014)
Hawkings, David T., *Pauper Ancestors: A Guide to The Records Created by The Poor Laws in England and Wales* (The History Press 2011)
Higginbotham, Peter, *The Workhouse Encyclopaedia* (The History Press 2014)
May, Trevor, *The Victorian Workhouse* (Shire Publications 1997)
Raymond, Stuart A., *Tracing your Poor Ancestors* (Pen and Sword 2020)
Stubley, Peter, *A Pauper's History of England: A 1000 Years of Peasants, Beggars and Guttersnipes* (Pen and Sword 2015)
Tate, W.E., *The Parish Chest* (Phillimore 3rd edition 2011)

National Archives' podcast *Living the Poor Life: Poverty and The Workhouse in the Nineteenth Century* Paul Carter **https://media.nationalarchives.gov.uk/index.php/living-the-poor-life-power-relations**

National Archives' research guide *Poverty and Poor Laws* **www.nationalarchives.gov.uk/help-with-your-research/research-guides/poverty-poor-laws**

National Archives' research guide *Workhouse Inmates and Staff* **www.nationalarchives.gov.uk/help-with-your-research/research-guides/workhouse-inmate-or-member-of-staff**

National Archives' research guide *Workhouses* **www.nationalarchives.gov.uk/help-with-your-research/research-guides/workhouse**

Overseers of the Poor Accounts **www.genguide.co.uk/source/overseers-of-the-poor-accounts-parish-amp-poor-law/97/**

Poor Law Records pre-1834 **www.familysearch.org/en/wiki/England_and_Wales_Poor_Law_Records_Pre-1834**

Poor Law and Rural Communities **www.mdlp.co.uk/resources/general/poor_law.htm**

Settlement **www.victorianweb.org/history/poorlaw/settle.html**

The Ragged School Museum **www.raggedschoolmuseum.org.uk**

Workhouses **www.workhouses.org.uk**

Selected sources for the case study of Harriet Bentlif

Census returns

General Registrar's indexes of birth, marriage and death

Tower Hamlets Cemetery, held at the London Metropolitan Archives, images available on Ancestry

Settlement examination and removal order St Luke's, Chelsea, held at the London Metropolitan Archives, images available on Ancestry

Records for Christ Church workhouse, Southwark, held at the London Metropolitan Archives, images available on Ancestry

Doctor Williams' Registry of Dissenters' Births

Fleet Prison entry books in class PRIS 10 at The National Archives, images available on Ancestry

London Evening Standard digitised by The British Newspaper Archive also be accessible via Findmypast

London Gazette **www.thegazette.co.uk**

Old Bailey Online **www.oldbaileyonline.org**

Chapter 2: Criminality
Further Reading

Hawkin, David T., *Criminal Ancestors: A Guide to Historical Criminal Records in England and Wales* (The History Press 2009) The eight appendices list hundreds of classes of criminal records and their whereabouts.

Park, Peter, *My Ancestors were Manorial Tenants* (Society of Genealogists 2002)

Stuart, Denis, *Manorial Records: An Introduction to Their Transcription and Translation* (Phillimore 2005)

Wade, Simon, *Tracing your Prisoner Ancestors: A Guide for Family Historians* (Pen and Sword 2020)

Waller, Ian, *Introducing Manorial Records: Unlocking the Mysteries of The Manor for Family Historians* (The Family History Partnership 2020)

Williams, Lucy, *Criminal Women 1850–1920: Researching the Lives of Britain's Female Offenders* (Pen and Sword (2018)

Williams, Lucy, *Wayward Women: Female Offending in Victorian England* (Pen and Sword 2016)

The British Newspaper Archive can also be accessed via Findmypast

Day, Chris *How to Trace your Criminal Ancestors* **https://blog.nationalarchives.gov.uk/trace-criminal-ancestors 2016**

Index to trials at the Central Criminal Court 1674–1913 **www.oldbaileyonline.org**

National Archives' research guide to researching Criminals and Convicts **www.nationalarchives.gov.uk/help-with-your-research/research-guides/criminals-and-convicts**

The Prison: the story of an institution **http://theprison.org.uk**

Scotland's Court and Criminal Database 1708–1909 **www.scottishindexes.com/ScotlandsCriminalDatabase.aspx**

Wayward Women: Victorian England's Female Offenders **https://waywardwomen.wordpress.com**

Selected sources for the case study of Frederick Michael Railton
General Registrar's indexes of birth, marriage and death

The marriage register of Bolton-le-Moors, Lancashire, held at Greater Manchester County Record Offices, images available on Ancestry

Census Returns

Newspaper reports digitised by the British Newspaper Archive can also be accessed via Findmypast

School Admissions' Registers for Salesbury Church of England School, held at Lancashire Archives, images available on Findmypast

Criminal Registers in class HO27 at The National Archives, images available on Findmypast and Ancestry

Habitual Criminals Register and Police Gazettes in class MEP06 at The National Archives, images available on Findmypast and Ancestry

The Calendar of Prisoners tried at the Assize, in class HO140 at The National Archives, images available on Findmypast and Ancestry

Index to Register of Prisoners in class PCOM2 at The National Archives, images available on Findmypast

Home Office and Prison Commission Male Licences in class PCOM3 at The National Archives, images available on Findmypast

Chapter 3: Ethnicity
Further Reading

Joseph, Anthony, *My Ancestors Were Jewish* (Society of Genealogists 4th edition 2008)

Kaufmann, Miranda, *Black Tudors: The Untold Story* (Oneworld Publications 2017)

Kerr, Barbara M., 'Irish Seasonal Migration to Great Britain 1800–1838' in *Irish Historical Studies* Vol. 3.12 September 1943 pp.365–380

Kershaw, Roger and Pearsall, Mark, *Immigrants and Aliens: A Guide to Sources on UK Immigration and Citizenship* (The National Archives 2004)

Kershaw, Roger, *Migration Records: A Guide for Family Historians* (The National Archives 2009)

Panayi, Panikos, *An Immigration History of Britain: Multicultural Racism Since 1800* (Routledge 2009)

Wenserul, Rosemary, *Tracing Your Jewish Ancestors: A Guide for Family Historians* (Pen and Sword 2008)

Ask about Ireland **www.askaboutireland.ie**

Avotaynu **www.avotaynu.com**

Bevis Marks Hall **www.bevismarks.org.uk**

Borthwick Institute research guide **www.york.ac.uk/borthwick/holdings/guides/research-guides/race/black-baptisms/**

E179 Database **www.nationalarchives.gov.uk/e179**

Lloyd, Amy J., *Emigration, Immigration and Migration in Nineteenth Century Britain* **www.gale.com/binaries/content/assets/gale-us-en/primary-sources/intl-gps/intl-gps-essays/full-ghn-contextual-essays/ghn_essay_bln_lloyd1_website.pdf**

England's Immigrants' Database **www.englandsimmigrants.com**

Jewish Genealogical Society of Great Britain **www.jgsgb.org.uk**

The Jewish Historical Society of England **www.jhse.org**

Jewish Museum **https://jewishmuseum.org.uk**

The Legacy of British Slave-ownership **www.ucl.ac.uk/lbs**

Manchester's Jewish Museum **www.manchesterjewishmuseum.com**

Migration Museum **www.migrationmuseum.org/exploring-the-migrant-history-of-victorian-east-london/**

Various National Archives research guides available for download at www.nationalarchives.gov.uk *Immigrants; Immigration; Jewish people and communities in Britain and its former colonies; Naturalisation*

and British Citizenship; Naturalised Britons; Nazi Persecution and the Holocaust; Refugees and Passport Records.
Our Migration Story **www.ourmigrationstory.org.uk**
Searching for Jamaican Families www.jamaicanfamilysearch.com/Samples/Registers.htm
Slave Voyages **www.slavevoyages.org**
Slavery and British Country Houses **https://historicengland.org.uk/images-books/publications/slavery-and-british-country-house/slavery-british-country-house-web/**
African Freedom in Tudor England **www.ourmigrationstory.uk/oms/african-freedom-in-tudor-england-dr-hector-nuness-request**
Switching the Lens Project **https://www.cityoflondon.gov.uk/things-to-do/history-and-heritage/london-metropolitan-archives/about-lma/switching-the-lens-project**
Windrush Stories **www.bl.uk/windrush**

Selected sources for the case study of Catherine Eve
The baptism register of Corsham, Wiltshire, held at Wiltshire and Swindon History Centre, images available on Findmypast
Slave Registers for 1813–1834 class T71 at The National Archives in class T71, images available on Ancestry
The Legacy of British Slave-ownership website **www.ucl.ac.uk/lbs/**

Chapter 4: Prostitution
Further reading
Hartley, Jenny, *Charles Dickens and the House of the Fallen Women* (Methuen 2009)
Hemyng, B., 'Prostitution in London', in Mayhew, H., *London Labour and the London Poor: Volume IV Those Who Will Not Work; Comprising Prostitutes, Thieves, Swindlers and Beggars* (Dover Publications 1862)
Flinders, Judith, *Prostitution* **www.bl.uk/romantics-and-victorians/articles/prostitution**
Joyce, Fraser, *Prostitution and the Nineteenth Century: In Search of the Great Social Evil.* **https://warwick.ac.uk/fac/cross_fac/iatl/reinvention/archive/volume1issue1/joyce**
Records of prostitution at the National Archives **https://discovery.nationalarchives.gov.uk/details/r/b4de3e9e-cf9b-477a-9935-c33b22a49a20**
Revisiting Dickens: prostitution in Victorian England
https://revisitingdickens.wordpress.com/prostitution-victorian/

Selected sources for the case study of Charity Platt
Index to the baptism register of Dalton-in-Furness, Lancashire, available on **www.familysearch.org**
General Registrar's indexes of birth, marriage and death
Census returns
1939 Register
Newspaper reports digitised by the British Newspaper Archive can also be accessed via Findmypast
Philip Martin's History Geek website **https://philmartin26.webador.co.uk/a-backdrop-of-history-on-china-street-lane-lancaster**
School admissions' register for Cambridge Primary Mixed School, Barrow-in-Furness, Cumbria, held at Barrow-in-Furness Record Office, images available on Findmypast
Prison Registers in class PCOM2 at The National Archives, images available on Findmypast
Habitual Criminals Register and Police Gazettes in class MEP06 at the National Archives, images available on Findmypast and Ancestry
The Calendar of Prisoners tried at the Assizes, in class HO140 at the National Archives images available on Findmypast and Ancestry

Chapter 5: Illegitimacy
Further Reading
Laslett, P. Oosterveen & Smith, R. M., *Bastardy and its Comparative History* (Edward Arnold 1980)
Levene, Alysa, *Childcare, Health and Mortality at The London Foundling Hospital, 1741–1800: Left to The Mercy of The World* (Manchester University Press 2007)
McClure, Ruth K., *Coram's Children: The London Foundling Hospital in the Eighteenth Century* (Yale University Press 1981)
Paley, Ruth, *My Ancestor Was a Bastard: A Family Historian's Guide to Sources for Illegitimacy in England and Wales* (Society of Genealogists 2011)
Children's Homes **www.childrenshomes.org.uk**
Voices through Time: the story of care **https://coramstory.org.uk/get-involved/creative-projects/**

Selected sources for the case study of Hannah Midgely
The parish registers of Tong, Yorkshire, held at West Yorkshire Archive Service, Bradford, images available on Findmypast
The parish registers of Birstall, Yorkshire, held at The Borthwick Institute, images available on Findmypast
Bastardy examinations and affiliation orders for Tong, Yorkshire, held in West Yorkshire Archive Service, images browsable on Ancestry

Chapter 6: The Inebriate
Further Reading
Dalrymple, D., 'Asylums for Drunkards', in *Macmillian's Magazine* xxvi pp.110–116 (1872)
Harrison, B., *Drink and the Victorians* (Faber & Faber, London 1971)
Morrison, Bronwyn, 'Inebriate Institutions', in Turner, Jo (ed.) *A Companion to the History of Crime and Criminal Justice* (Policy Press 2017) pp.110–111
Putnam, Roger, *The Beer and Breweries of Britain* (Shire Books 2004)
Wilson, G., *Alcohol and the Nation* (Nicholson and Watson 1940)
Winskill, Peter Turner, *The Comprehensive History of the Rise and Progress of the Temperance Reformation from the Earliest Period to September 1881* (Mackie Brewtnall 1881)
The British Women's Temperance Association (now the White Ribbon Association) **https://white-ribbon.org.uk/our-history/**
Drunk and Riotous: troubled and troublesome inebriate women **https://lesleyhulonce.wordpress.com/2015/07/15/drunk-and-riotous-troubled-and-troublesome-inebriate-women/**
Government enquiry into the history of alcoholism **https://publications.parliament.uk/pa/cm200910/cmselect/cmhealth/151/15106.htm**
The Temple Lodge Home for Inebriate Women, Torquay, Devon **https://inebriateancestors.co.uk**

Select sources for the case study of Sarah Grosvenor
West Midlands Prisoner Photo Book, held at the West Midlands Police Museum, images available on Ancestry
Calendar of Prisoners 1890 and 1892 HO 140 at The National Archives, images available on Findmypast and Ancestry
Criminal Register 1890 St Mary's Newington Court HO27 216 at The National Archives, images available on Ancestry
Criminal Register 1892 St Mary's Newington Court HO27 222 at The National Archives, images available on Ancestry
General Registrar's indexes of birth, marriage and death
Census returns
Newspaper reports digitised by the British Newspaper Archive can also be accessed via Findmypast

Chapter 7: Sickness and Disability
Further Reading
Abel-Smith, Brian, *The Hospitals: 1800–1948: A Study in Social Administration in England and Wales* (Heinemann 1964)
Black, N., *Walking London's Medical History* (Royal Society of Medicine Press 2006)

Cummings, Juliana, *Medicine in the Middle Ages: Surviving the Times* (Pen and Sword 2021)

Dainton, Courtney, *The Story of England's Hospitals* (London Museum Press 1961)

Few, Janet, *'Til Death Us Do Part: Causes of Death 1300–1948* (Unlock the Past 2015)

Gerard, John, *Gerard's Herbal* (1994 Studio Editions Limited (originally published in 1633))

Grundy, Joan, *A Dictionary of Medical and Related Terms for the Family Historian* (Family History Partnership 2006)

Jarrett, Simon, *A History of Disability in England from the Medieval Period to the Present Day* (Liverpool University Press 2023)

Jarrett, Simon, *Those They Called Idiots: The Idea of The Disabled Mind from 1700 to the Present Day* (Reaktion Books 2020)

McGann, Stephen, *Flesh and Blood: A History of My Family in Seven Sicknesses* (Simon and Schuster 2018)

Norman, Ben, *A History of Death in Seventeenth Century England* (Pen and Sword 2020)

Raymond, Stuart, *Death and Burial Records for Family Historians* (Family History Partnership 2011)

Read, Sara and Evans, Jennifer, *Maladies and Medicine: Exploring Health and Healing 1540–1750* (Pen and Sword 2017)

Richardson, John, *The Local Historian's Encyclopaedia* (3rd ed. Historical Publications Ltd. 2003)

Ryan T., *The History of Queen Charlotte's Lying-In Hospital* (1885)

Webb, Cliff, *An Index of London Hospitals and their Records* (Society of Genealogists 2002)

Wills, Simon, *How our Ancestors Died: A Guide for Family Historians* (Pen and Sword 2013)

Analysis of English and Welsh 1871 census disabilities **www.thesocialhistorian.com/blind-deaf-and-dumb-imbecile-or-lunatic**

Bills of Mortality http://wellcomelibrary.org/item/b20663717#?c=0&m=0&s=0&cv=0&z=-0.1377%2C-0.0718%2C1.2753%2C1.4363

The Casebook of John Westover Surgeon 1686–1700 www.tutton.org/content/Westover_journal.pdf

Culpeper's Herbal https://archive.org/details/culpeperscomplet00culpuoft

Dene Hollow Oral School for the Deaf https://blog.nationalarchives.gov.uk/the-dene-hollow-oral-school-for-the-deaf/

Epidemics Timeline https://awfhs.org/hub/epidemics-timeline

Epidemics Timeline www.hyattfamily.co.uk/docs/General%20genealogy%20help/british%20epidemic%20timeline.txt

Folk Remedies www.historic-uk.com/CultureUK/Folk-Remedies
A History of Disability https://historicengland.org.uk/research/inclusive-heritage/disability-history/
The Historical Hospital Admissions Records' Project www.hharp.org
The History of Disability https://historicengland.org.uk/research/inclusive-heritage/disability-history/
HMS Dreadnought Seaman's Hospital Admissions 1826–1920 www.zooniverse.org/projects/msalmon/hms-nhs-the-nautical-health-service
Hospitals, Asylums and Sanatoriums (worldwide) from Cyndi's List www.cyndislist.com/medical/hospitals/
The Hospital Records' hospital records database www.nationalarchives.gov.uk/hospitalrecords/
Jarrett, Simon, *Disability in Time and Place* https://historicengland.org.uk/content/docs/research/disability-in-time-and-place-pdf/
Jarrett, Simon, *He is so Silly he would Rather have a Half Pence than a Shilling: discovering the history of learning disability* https://media.nationalarchives.gov.uk/index.php/discovering-the-history-of-learning-disability/
Lost Hospitals of London http://ezitis.myzen.co.uk
Medical Officer of Health Reports https://archive.org/details/medicalofficerofhealthreports
Medical Officer of Health Reports for London boroughs from 1848 to 1972 http://wellcomelibrary.org/moh
Mortality Statistics http://wellcomelibrary.org/collections/subject-guides/introduction-to-mortality-statistics-in-england-and-wales/#anchor1
www.ons.gov.uk/peoplepopulationandcommunity/birthsdeathsandmarriages/deaths/articles/causesofdeathover100years/2017–09–18
National Archives' guide *Disability History* www.nationalarchives.gov.uk/help-with-your-research/research-guides/disability-history/
Representative Medical Records of Servicemen www.scarletfinders.co.uk/125.html
The Royal Society of Medicine Library www.rsm.ac.uk/library/
Timeline of Anesthesia www.woodlibrarymuseum.org/history-of-anesthesia
Voluntary Hospitals' Database www.hospitalsdatabase.lshtm.ac.uk
Wesley, John, *Primitive Physick* http://books.google.co.uk/books?id=fLEUAAAAQAAJ&printsec=frontcover&dq=John+Wesley+primitive+physick
Woodall, John, *The Surgeon's Mate* https://archive.org/details/surgionsmateortr00wood

Selected sources for the case study of Richard Gill and William Leathern
General Registrar's indexes of birth, marriage and death
Death certificates
Census returns
Admissions' Register for Exminster Asylum
Records of the Barnstaple Bible Christian Circuit
Workhouse Register of Lunatics at Torrington workhouse

Chapter 8: The Mentally Ill
Further Reading
Arnold, Catharine, *Bedlam: London and its Mad* (Simon & Schuster 2009)
Burtinshaw, Kathryn, & Burt, Dr John, *Lunatics, Imbeciles and Idiots: A History of Insanity in Nineteenth Century Britain and Ireland* (Pen and Sword 2017)
Burtinshaw, Kathryn, & Burt, Dr John, *Madness, Murder and Mayhem: Criminal Insanity in Victorian and Edwardian Britain* (Pen and Sword 2018)
Chambers, Paul, *Bedlam: London's Hospital for the Mad* (Ian Allen Publishing 2009)
Chater, Kathy, *My Ancestor was a Lunatic: A Guide to Sources for Family Historians* (Society of Genealogists 2014)
Costello, Victoria, *A Lethal Inheritance: A Mother Uncovers the Science Behind Three Generations of Mental Illness* (Prometheus Books 2012)
Davis, Mark, *Voices from the Asylum: West Riding Pauper Lunatic Asylum* (Amberley Publishing 2013)
Davis, Mark, *Asylum: Inside the Pauper Lunatic Asylums* (Amberley Publishing 2019)
Finnane, Mark, *Insanity and the Insane in Post-famine Ireland* (Rowman & Littlefield 1981)
Grogan, Susie, *Shell-shocked Britain: The First World War's Legacy for Britain's Mental Health* (Pen and Sword 2014)
Higgs, Michelle, *Tracing your Ancestors in Lunatic Asylums: A Guide for Family Historians* (Pen and Sword 2019)
Houston, R.A., *Madness and Society in Eighteenth Century Scotland* (OUP 2000)
Ingram, Allan, (ed.) *Patterns of Madness in the Eighteenth Century: A Reader* (Liverpool University Press 1998)
Jones, Kathleen, *Law and Conscience, 1744–1845: The Social History of the Care of the Insane* (Routledge & Kegan Paul 1955)
MacDonald, M., *Mystical Bedlam: Madness, Anxiety and Healing in Seventeenth Century England* (2nd edition Cambridge University Press 1983)

Parry-Jones, William Llywelyn, *The Trade in Lunacy: A Study of Private Madhouses in England in the Eighteenth and Nineteenth Century* (Routledge 1972)

Reid, Fiona, *Broken Men: Shellshock, Treatment and Recovery in Britain 1914–1930* (Continuum 2010)

Scull, Andrew T., *Museums of Madness: The Social Organisation of Insanity in Nineteenth Century England* (Viking 1979)

Stevens, Mark, *Broadmoor Revisited: Victorian Crime and The Lunatic Asylum* (Pen and Sword 2013)

Stevens, Mark, *Life in the Victorian Asylum: The World of Nineteenth Century Mental Health Care* (Pen and Sword 2014)

Winslow, Lyttleton Stuart Forbes, *Manual of Lunacy: A Handbook Relating to The Legal Care and Treatment of the Insane in Britain, Ireland, United States of America and The Continent* (Cambridge University Press 2014)

Wise, Sarah, *Inconvenient People: Lunacy, Liberty and the Mad Doctors in Victorian England* (Vintage 2013)

County Asylums **www.countyasylums.co.uk**

England's First Asylums **www.sochealth.co.uk/national-health-service/hospitals/englands-first-state-imbecile-asylums**

History Co-operative Mental Illness **http://historycooperative.org/a-beautiful-mind-thc-history-of-the-treatment-of-mental-illness**

The History of the Asylum **http://thetimechamber.co.uk/beta/sites/asylums/asylum-history/the-history-of-the-asylum**

The History of The Retreat **https://theretreatyork.org.uk/our-history/**

Hospitals, Asylums and Sanatoriums (worldwide) from Cyndi's List **www.cyndislist.com/medical/hospitals/**

Index of English and Welsh Lunatic Asylums and Mental Hospitals. Based on a comprehensive survey of 1844 and extended to other asylums **http://studymore.org.uk/4_13_TA.HTM**

There is also a guide to *Asylums, Psychiatric Hospitals and Mental Health* **www.nationalarchives.gov.uk/help-with-your-research/research-guides/mental-health/**

On the Periphery: A Survey of Nineteenth-Century Asylums in the United States **https://tigerprints.clemson.edu/cgi/viewcontent.cgi?referer=https://www.google.co.uk/&httpsredir=1&article=3128&context=all_theses**

Scottish Asylum Patients **www.oldscottish.com/asylum-patients.html**

Selected sources for the case study of Fanny Amelia Ellington
Birth, marriage and death certificates
General Registrar's indexes of birth, marriage and death
Census returns

Baptism register for Highgate, Middlesex, held at London Metropolitan Archives, images available on Ancestry

Admissions' Register for Workhouse, Constance Road, East Dulwich, Surrey, held at London Metropolitan Archives CABG/185/31 and CABG/185/40, images available on Ancestry

Admissions' Registers for the Asylums and Psychiatric Hospitals of the Lunacy Commission and Board of Control MH94 at The National Archives, images available on Ancestry

Cane Hill Asylum, Coulsdon, Surrey www.countyasylums.co.uk/cane-hill-coulsdon

Constance Road Workhouse www.workhouses.org.uk/Camberwell/

Horton Asylum www.countyasylums.co.uk/horton-asylum-epsom

Julius Wagner-Jauregg (1857–1940): Introducing fever therapy in the treatment of neurosyphilis www.ncbi.nlm.nih.gov/pubmed/24185088

Chapter 9: The Romany and Traveller Community
Further Reading

Floate, Sharon, *My Ancestors were Gypsies* (Society of Genealogists 3 edition 2010)

Keet-Black, Janet, *Gypsies of Britain* (Shire 2013)

Loveridge, Pat, *Calendar of Fairs and Markets Held in the Nineteenth Century* (Romany and Traveller Family History Society 2003)

'Am I Descended from Gypsies?' *Who do you Think you Are*? Magazine article www.whodoyouthinkyouaremagazine.com/tutorials/am-i-descended-from-gypsies

Fairground Heritage Trust www.fairground-heritage.org.uk

Gordon Boswell's Romany Museum www.romaniarts.co.uk/the-boswell-romany-museum/

Access to Gypsy Lore Society Journals https://catalog.hathitrust.org/Record/000499763

Their archives are held at Liverpool University Library

National Fairground and Circus Archive is held by the University of Sheffield www.sheffield.ac.uk/nfca

RomArchive www.romarchive.eu/en/

Romani Diaspora www.wikiwand.com/en/Romani_diaspora#/overview

Romany and Traveller Family History Society http://rtfhs.org.uk/

Romany Wales www.valleystream.co.uk/romhome.htm

Selected sources for the case study of Joshua Mobbs
General Registrar's indexes of birth, marriage and death
Census returns

The baptism registers of Lissington, Lincolnshire, held at Lincolnshire Archives, images available on Findmypast

The baptism registers of Market Rasen, Lincolnshire, held at Lincolnshire Archives, images available on Findmypast

Newspaper reports digitised by the British Newspaper Archive can also be accessed via Findmypast

Criminal Registers in class HO27 at The National Archives, images available on Findmypast and Ancestry

Calendar of Prisons to be tried at the Quarter Session in class HO140 at The National Archives, images available on Findmypast and Ancestry

Chapter 10: Witchcraft
Further Reading

Caporael, Linnda, 'Ergotism: The Satan Loosed in Salem?' in *Science* 192, no. 4234 (1976) pp.21–26

Davies, Owen, *Cunning Folk: Popular Magic in English History* (Hambledon Continuum 2007)

Gaskill, Malcolm, *Witchfinders: A Seventeenth Century English Tragedy* (John Murray 2005)

MacFarlane, Alan, *Witchcraft in Tudor and Stuart England: A Regional and Comparative Study* (Routledge 1970)

Martin, Lois, *The History of Witchcraft* (Pocket Essentials 2007)

Maxwell-Stuart, P.G., *Witchcraft a History* (Tempus Publishing Ltd. 2000)

Notestein, Wallace, *History of Witchcraft in England from 1558 to 1718* (Benediction Classics 2012)

Sharpe, James, *Instruments of Darkness: Witchcraft in Early Modern England* (University of Pennsylvania Press 1997)

Winsham, Willow, *Accused: British Witches Throughout History* (Pen and Sword 2016)

Winsham, Willow, *England's Witchcraft Trials* (Pen and Sword 2018)

Cunning Folk **www.karisgarden.co.uk/cunningfolk**

List of English witch trials **www.witchtrials.co.uk**. Although this site is ostensibly about the Essex witch trials, it contains a great deal of general information including details of the witchcraft acts and a long list of those tried for witchcraft in Essex.

The Salem witch trials **https://salemwitchtrialsresearch.wordpress.com**

Seventeenth-century witchcraft in Flintshire, at the National Library of Wales website **www.llgc.org.uk/index.php?id=witchcraftcourtofgrearsessi**

Survey of Scottish Witchcraft **www.shc.ed.ac.uk/Research/witches**

The UK parliament site has an overview of laws against witchcraft in England at **www.parliament.uk/about/living-heritage/transformingsociety/private-lives/religion/overview/witchcraft/**
Witchcraft legislation **www.parliament.uk/about/living-heritage/transformingsociety/private-lives/religion/overview/witchcraft/**
Witches in Early Modern England **http://witching.org**
Witchcraft in Elizabeth England **www.elizabethan-era.org.uk/elizabethan-witchcraft-and-witches.htm**

Selected sources for the case study of Susanna Edwards
Anon. *A True and impartial relation of the informations against three witches, viz., Temperance Lloyd, Mary Trembles, and Susanna Edwards, who were indicted, arraigned and convicted at the assizes holden for the county of Devon, at the castle of Exon, Aug. 14, 1682 with their several confessions, taken before Thomas Gist, Mayor, and John Davie, alderman, of Biddiford, in the said county, where they were inhabitants : as also, their speeches, confessions and behaviour at the time and place of execution on the twenty fifth of the said month* (Freeman Collins 1682)
Baring-Gould, Sabine, *The Bideford Witches and other tales of Devonshire Witchcraft* (Cunning Crime Books 2012)
Barry, Jonathan, *Witchcraft and Demonism in South West England: Palgrave Historical Studies in Witchcraft and Magic* (Palgrave Macmillan 2012)
Few, Janet, *Sins as Red as Scarlet* (Blue Poppy Publishing 2020) a fictionalised account of Susanna and her co-accused.
Fraser, Antonia, *The Weaker Vessel: Woman's Lot in Seventeenth Century England* (Weidenfeld & Nicolson 1984)
Gent, Frank J., *The Trial of the Bideford Witches* (Crediton Gent 1982)
Granville, Rev. Preb. R., *A History of the Church at Bideford and some of its Rectors* Report and Transactions of The Devonshire Association (1902) Vol. 34 pp. 201–222
Stagg, Kevin, *Port in a Storm: Witchcraft and Immunity in Restoration Bideford* unpublished MA thesis Cardiff University (unknown date)
Timmons, Stephen, 'Witchcraft and Rebellion in late seventeenth-century Devon', in *Journal of Modern History* 10 (2006)
Watkins, John, *An Essay Towards a History of Bideford in the County of Devon* (Lazarus Publishing 1993) (originally published 1792) available as a free ebook
https://books.google.co.uk/books/about/An_Essay_Towards_a_History_of_Bideford_i.html?id=iW9bAAAAQAAJ
The parish registers of Bideford, Devon, held at North Devon Record Office, images available on Findmypast
Bideford Sessions of the Peace Book 1659–1709, held at North Devon Record Office

Chapter 11: Other Marginalised Groups
Further Reading
Religious Belief
Bourne, F.W., *The Bible Christians: Their Origins and History 1815–1900* (2nd edition Tentmaker Publications 2004)
Breed, G.R., *My Ancestors were Baptists* (Society of Genealogists 1986)
Brown, Kenneth D., A Social History of the Nonconformist Ministry in England and Wales 1800–1930 (Clarendon Press 1988)
Clifford, David, *My Ancestors were Congregationalists* (Society of Genealogists 1998)
Gandy, Michael, *Catholic Family History: A Bibliography of Local Sources* (Michael Gandy 1996)
Gandy, Michael, *Catholic Missions and Registers 1700–1880* (6 vols. and atlas vol. Michael Gandy 1993)
Hempton, David, *Religion and Political Culture in Britain and Ireland* (Cambridge University Press 1996)
Holt, Geoffrey, *The English Jesuits 1650–1829: A Biographical Dictionary* (Catholic Record Society record series 70 1984)
Leary, William, *My Ancestors Were Methodists: How Can I Find Out More About Them?* (Society of Genealogists 1993)
Milligan, Edward H. and Thomas, Malcolm J., *My Ancestors were Quakers* (2nd ed. Society of Genealogists 1999)
Ratcliffe, Richard, *Basic Facts About the Wesleyan Methodist Historic Roll* (Federation of Family History Societies 2005)
Ruston, Alan, *My Ancestors were English Presbyterians & Unitarians: How Can I Find Out More About Them?* (Society of Genealogists 2001)
Shaw, Thomas, *The Bible Christians 1815–1907* (Epworth Press 1965)
Snape, Michael Francis, 'Anti-Methodism in Eighteenth-Century England: The Pendle Forest Riots of 1748', in *Journal of Ecclesiastical History* Vol. 49.2 April 1998 pp. 257–281
Tiller, Kate, *The Desert Begins to Blossom: Oxfordshire and Primitive Methodism 1824–1860* available at **http://oxoniensia.org/volumes/2006/tiller.pdf**
Towey, Peter, *My Ancestor was an Anglican Clergyman* (Society of Genealogists 2006)
Waller, Ian, *My Ancestor was a Mormon* (Society of Genealogists 2012)
Whiteman Annie, (ed.) *The Compton Census of 1676: A Critical Edition* (Oxford University Press 1986)
Wiggins J.R., *My Ancestors were in the Salvation Army* (Society of Genealogists 1999)
Williams, J. Anthony, *Recusant History: Sources for Recusant History (1559 To 1791) in English Official Archives* (Catholic Record Society 1983)
Archbishopric of York **https://archbishopsregisters.york.ac.uk**

British Religion in Numbers including access to 1851 census **www.brin.ac.uk/2010/religious-census-1851-online/**

The Clergy of the Church of England Database (CCEd) **www.theclergydatabase.org.uk**

Crockford's Clerical Directory **www.crockford.org.uk**

The Dissenting Experience **https://dissent.hypotheses.org/**

Dr Williams' Library **https://dwl.ac.uk**

Fasti Ecclesiae Anglicanae gives details of all the higher clergy of the Church of England from early times to the mid-nineteenth century **www.british-history.ac.uk/catalogue.aspx?gid=157**

The Genealogist **www.thegenealogist.co.uk**

Historic England Guide to Non-conformist Places of Worship **https://historicengland.org.uk/images-books/publications/iha-nonconformist-places-of-worship/**

An Inventory of Puritan and Dissenting Records 1640–1714 **www.qmul.ac.uk/sed/religionandliterature/online-publications/dissenting-records/**

The National Archives Guide *Non-conformist Records* **www.nationalarchives.gov.uk/help-with-your-research/research-guides/nonconformist-non-parish-births-marriages-deaths-1567–1969/**

The Official Non-Conformist and Non-Parochial BMDs website **www.bmdregisters.co.uk**

Religious Census 1851 **http://discovery.nationalarchives.gov.uk/browse/r/h/C8993**

Religious Persecution **www.parliament.uk/about/living-heritage/transformingsociety/private-lives/religion/overview/persecution/**

Baptists

Angus Library of Baptist History **http://anguslibraryandarchive.blogspot.co.uk/**

The Baptist Historical Society **www.baptisthistory.org.uk**

Catholics

The Catholic Archives Society **www.catholicarchivesociety.org**

The Catholic Family History Society **http://catholicfhs.online/**

Catholic Record Society **www.catholicrecordsociety.co.uk**

The Centre for Catholic Studies **www.dur.ac.uk/theology.religion/ccs/**

The National Archives Guide to Catholic Research **www.nationalarchives.gov.uk/help-with-your-research/research-guides/catholics/**

Methodism

John Rylands Library **www.library.manchester.ac.uk/rylands**

Methodist Central Hall **www.methodist-central-hall.org.uk**
Methodist Heritage **www.methodistheritage.org.uk**
My Methodist History **www.MyMethodistHistory.org.uk**
My Primitive Methodist Ancestors **www.MyPrimitiveMethodists.org.uk**
My Wesleyan Methodist Ancestors **www.MyWesleyanMethodists.org.uk**
The Wesley Historical Society **www.wesleyhistoricalsociety.org.uk**

Bible Christians
The Bible Christian Project co-ordinates research, more information can be found here **http://freepages.history.rootsweb.ancestry.com/~biblechristian/**
My Bible Christians **www.mybiblechristians.org.uk**

Quakers
The Friends Historical Society **https://friendshistoricalsociety.org.uk/**
The Quaker Family History Society **www.qfhs.co.uk**
Society of Friends Library **www.quaker.org.uk/library**

Judaism
See Chapter 3

Huguenots
The Huguenot Society **www.huguenotsociety.org.uk**

Other non-conformists
Churches Conservation Trust **www.visitchurches.org.uk**
Moravian church archives see **www.moravian.org.uk/who-we-are/church-archives**
United Reformed Church History Society **www.urc.org.uk** (Presbyterians and Congregationalists)

Sexuality
Bray, A., *Homosexuality in Renaissance England* (Columbia University Press 1996)
Buckle, Sebastian, *The Way Out: A History of Homosexuality in Modern Britain* (I B Tauris 2015)
Cant, B. and Hemmings, S., (eds) *Radical Records: Thirty Years of Lesbian and Gay History, 1957–1987* (Routledge 1988)
Cook, M. with Mills, R., Trumbach, R., and Cocks, H.G., *A Gay History of Britain: Love and Sex Between Men Since the Middle Ages* (Greenwood World Publishing 2007)
David, H., *On Queer Street: A Social History of British Homosexuality, 1895–1995* (Harper Collins 1997)

Donoghue, E., *Passions Between Women: British Lesbian Culture, 1668–1801* (Bello 2014)

Jennings, Rebecca, *A Lesbian History of Britain* (Greenwood World Publishing 2007)

Lesbian History Group (ed.) *Not a Passing Phase: Reclaiming Lesbians in History, 1840–1985* (Women's Press 1989)

Marcus, S., *Between Women: Friendship, Desire, and Marriage in Victorian England* (Princeton 2007)

Oram, A., *'Her Husband Was a Woman!': Women's Gender Crossing in Modern British Popular Culture* (Routledge 2007)

Oram, A. and Turnbull, A., *The Lesbian History Sourcebook: Love and Sex between Women in Britain from 1780 to 1970* (Routledge 2001)

Rossini, Gill, *Same Sex Love 1700–1957: A History and Research Guide* (Pen and Sword 2017)

England's LQBTQ Heritage **https://historicengland.org.uk/research/inclusive-heritage/lgbtq-heritage-project/**

Lesbian and Gay News Media Archive **www.lagna.org.uk**

LGBTQ History **www.english-heritage.org.uk/learn/histories/lgbtq-history/**

Findmypast Guide *How to Trace LGBT Ancestors* **www.findmypast.co.uk/blog/help/lgbt-ancestors**

Timeline of LGBTQ History in Britain **www.bl.uk/lgbtq-histories/lgbtq-timeline**

Conscientious Objection and Desertion

Bales, Mitzi, *They said 'No' to War: British Women Conscientious Objectors in World War II* **https://wri-irg.org/en/story/2010/they-said-no-war-british-women-conscientious-objectors-world-war-ii**

Barker, Rachel, *Conscience, Government and War* (Routledge and Kegan Paul, 1982)

Ellsworth-Jones, Will, *We Will Not Fight* (Aurum Press Ltd. 2008)

Gregory, Susan, *The South West Tribunal: Conscientious Objectors in WWII* **www.brh.org.uk/site/articles/the-south-west-tribunal**

Kennedy, Thomas, *The Hound of Conscience: A History of the No-Conscription Fellowship, 1914–1919* (University of Arkansas Press 1981)

McDermott, James, *British Military Service Tribunals 1916–1918* (Manchester University Press 2011)

Spencer, William, *Family History in the Wars* (The National Archives 2007)

Appeal tribunals for Middlesex **www.nationalarchives.gov.uk**

Conscientious Objectors in their own Words Imperial War Museum **www.iwm.org.uk/history/conscientious-objectors-in-their-own-words**

Everyday Lives in War: conscientious objectors **https://everydaylivesinwar.herts.ac.uk/tag/conscientious-objectors/**

Friends' Ambulance Service **http://fau.quaker.org.uk**
Harringay Peace Forum **https://hfwwpf.wordpress.com**
The Men Who Said No: conscientious objectors 1915–1919 **www.menwhosaidno.org/context/context_ncfIntro.html**
National Archives Guide *Researching Conscientious Objectors* **www.nationalarchives.gov.uk/help-with-your-research/research-guides/conscientious-objectors**
Voices of the First World War: conscientious objection **www.iwm.org.uk/history/voices-of-the-first-world-war-conscientious-objection**

Selected sources for the case study of William Wilcox
Birth and Death Certificates
General Registrar's indexes of marriage
Census returns
Statement of Army Service, original at The National Archives WO97 4161/1187
The Hartland Chronicle 15 March 1905 p. 27 col. a

INDEX

Abbott, Ellen, 37
Abbott, Peter, 36
Abbott, Peter Harris, 36
Abolition of slavery, 36
Abortion, 46–7, 53
Acts of Parliament:
   Againste Conjuracons, Inchantments and Witchcraftes, 107
   Alehouse Act, 59
   Aliens Act, 33
   Beerhouses Act, 60
   Buggery Act, 119
   Contagious Diseases Acts, 43
   County Asylums Act, 86
   Criminal Law Amendment Act, 118
   Defence of the Realm Act, 62
   Egyptians' Act, 96
   Family Law Reform Act, 56
   Friendly Societies Act, 76
   Gilbert's Act, 5
   Habeus Corpus Act, 24
   Habitual Drunkards' Licensing Act, 62
   Inebriates Act, 61
   Knatchbull Act, 5
   Legitimacy Act, 56
   Lunatics Act, 83
   Madhouses Act, 85
   Mental Deficiency Act, 78
   Military Service Act, 120, 122–3
   Military Training Act, 121
   Non-parochial Registers Act, 116
   Offences Against the Person Act, 53, 119
   Poor Law Amendment Act, 5, 55, 78
   Poor Law, Elizabethan, 3, 77
   Poor Law or 1576, 52
   Prevention of Cruelty to Children Act, 62
   Public Health Act, 76
   Punishment of Sturdy Vagabonds and Beggars, 96
   Repression of Vagrancy, 2
   Settlement, 8
   Sunday Closing Act, 61
   Supplying some Defects in the Laws for the Relief of the Poor of this Kingdom, Act for, 3
   Toleration Act, 114
   Vagrancy Act, 1, 97
   Workhouse Test Act, 4–5

Adams, Margaret, 53–4
Aldersgate, Middlesex, 115
Alexandra Hospital for Children
    with Hip Disease, 75
Aliens, 30–3
    arrivals, 33
    entry books, 33
    subsidies, 32
Alleged Lunatics Friends'
    Society, 86
Allen, Anne, 52
Allen, Elener, 2
Allen, John, 2
Allwood, Rev. Robert, 36
Allwood, Robert, 36
Amputation, 72–3
Anaesthesia, 72–3
Anderson, Charles, 66
Antenuptial Relationship Index, 55
Antibiotics, 73
Anti-semitism, 29, 33, 114
Ashmore, John, 54
Aspin, Elizabeth, 46
Assisted passage schemes, 11
Asylums, 78, 85–7
Axford, Maurice, 76

Bacon, Roger, 69
Badging the poor, 2–3
Bailey, Thomas, 121
Baker, Mr., 12
Band of Hope, 62
Barber surgery, 72, 74
Barnes, Grace, 110
Barnes, John, 110
Barnstaple, Devon, 32
Barrow, Lancashire, 48
Basson, Thomas, 52
Bastardy:
    bonds, 52
    examinations, 52–3, 56
    legislation, 52
Beare, Dr, 110

Beare, Mary, 111
Benift of the clergy, 19–20
Bennett, Sarah, 65
Bentley, Derek, 19
Bentlif, Amelia, 12
Bentlif, Charles, 12
Bentlif, David, 12
Bentlif, Edward, 12–13
Bentlif, George, 12–13
Bentlif, Harriet, 12–13
Bentlif, Sarah Godfrey, 12
Bermondsey, Surrey, 12–13
Bethlehem Royal Hospital, 84
Bevis Marks Hall, 34
Bible Christian church, 80
Bicknell, Lieutenant, 20
Bideford, Devon, 110–12
Bills of mortality, 74–5
Birch, Ann, 41
Birmingham, Warwickshire, 62, 64–7
Birstall, Yorkshire, 56
Bishops' visitations, 109
Black Death, 33
Black, Jacobus, 32
Blackburn, Lancashire, 25–8
Blackpool, Lancashire, 49
Blandford Forum, Dorset, 11
Blood loss, 73
Bloody Code, The, 19
Blundle, John, 35
Blyborough, Lincolnshire, 100
Bolton, Lancashire, 28
Bolton-le-Moors, Lancashire, 25
Borthwick Institute, 17, 90
Boswell family, 101
Bowron, William, 49
Bowskill, John, 15
Bradford, Yorkshire, 56–7
Braund, George Harold, 120
Braybrooke, George, 15
Bremmicombe, Thomas, 112
Brereton-cum-Smethwick,
    Cheshire, 52

Brighstone, Isle of Wight, 3–4
British Lying-in Hospital,
    Holborn, 75
British Newspaper Archive, 14
Broadmoor prison, 80
Broadwindsor, Dorset, 53
Brooks, Mabel, 62
Brothels, 41, 44–5, 47–9
Brown, Agnes, 55
Brown, Harriet, 100
Brown, Henry, 118
Buckley, Catherine, 42
Buckley, George, 41
Burney, Fanny, 72
Bush, Ann Rebecca, 36
Bush, Joseph, 36
Buxton, Madam, 35

Caddy, Elizabeth, 111
Calendar of prisoners, 26, 49,
    65–6, 100
Callistock. Dorset, 10
Camberwell, Surrey, 91
Cane Hill Pauper Lunatic
    Asylum, 92
Cape of Good Hope,
    South Africa, 124
Cardell, Mary, 90
Cardiff, Glamorganshire, 124
Carlisle, Ann, 62
Carlisle, Cumberland, 63
Carter, Joseph, 118
Casual wards, 7
Cawkivell, Thomas, 88
Cerne, Dorset, 10
Charles II, 40
Chartists, 62
Chatham, Kent, 124
Chertsey, Surrey, 92
Church of England Temperance
    Society, 63
Clamp, Benjamin, 48–9
Coleman, Dorcas, 110–12

College of Arms, 35
Compton, Henry, 116
Compton, Jane, 83
Connor, Hannah, 20
Conscientious objectors, 119–24
    Register, 121
Cook, John, 57
Cooke, Jonathan, 52
Coram, Thomas, 54
Corsham, Wiltshire, 38–9
Court Baron, 17
Courts, 15–17
    Assize Courts, 16
    Central Criminal Court, 12, 16,
        22–4, 53
    Chancery, 16, 89
    Common Pleas, 16
    Crown Courts, 16–17
    Exchequer, 16
    High Court of Justiciary, 17
    King's Bench, 16
    Kirk Sessions, 55
    Magistrates' Courts, 16–17
    Manorial Courts, 15, 17
    Old Bailey, see Central Criminal
        Court
    Petty Sessions, 15, 55
    Quarter Sessions, 11, 15–16, 22,
        33, 53, 60, 90, 98, 100, 109
    Queen's Bench, 16
    Sheriff's Courts, 17
    Star Chamber, 16
    Supreme Court of Judicature, 16
Criminal lunacy and warrant
    entry books, 88
Criminal lunatic asylum
    registers, 88
Criminal petitions, 24
Criminal registers, 15, 100
Cromwell, Oliver, 33, 97
Crooks, William, 49
Culmstock, Devon, 10
Culpeper, Nicholas, 74

Dagenham, Essex, 88
Dalrymple, Dr, 60
Dalton-in Furnace, Lancashire, 47–9
Dartmouth, Devon, 32
Davy, Humphrey, 73
Dearling, W.H., 65
Death certificates, 74
Death clubs, 76
Death penalty, 19, 107, 119
Dedham, Essex, 52
Denizations, 30–2
Deserters, 123–4
Dickens, Charles, 40
Digbeth, Warwickshire, 66
Disability, 76–9
Diskell, Mary Ann, 10
Dissolution of the monasteries, 1, 73, 77
DNA, 37–8, 50, 95
Doctrine of signatures, 70
Dodds, Ralph, 118
Dolton, Devon, 125
Dore, John, 4
Dover, Kent, 124
Dowland, John James Golden, 53
Dr Williams' Register, 12
Driscoll, Morris, 52
Driscoll, Sarah, 52
Driscoll, William Henry, 51
Dudley, Worcestershire, 64–7
Dulwich, Surrey, 91
Dunlop, John, 62
Dunning, John, 111
Dyett, Frances Maria, 37

Earlswood, Surrey, 78
Early closing movement, 45
East Compton, Dorset, 10
East India Company, 89
Ecclesiastical census, 34, 116
Ecclesiastical courts, 17–18, 53
Edgar, Dr, 62

Edinburgh, Scotland, 17, 118, 121
Edward VII, 41
Edwards, David, 110
Edwards, Susanna, 110–13
Edwards, William, 111
Elizabeth, 35
Ellington, Fanny Amelia, 90–2
Ellington, George Frederick, 90, 92
Ellington, Richard Collings Stanley 90
Ellington, William, 90–1
Ellis, Ruth, 19
Ellwood, Thomas, 115
Emma, 37
England's Immigrants Database, 32
Enslavement, 35–9
Etherly, Durham, 118
Eugenics, 29, 78
Evans, Timothy, 19
Eve, Catherine, 38–9
Evelina Hospital, 75
Exeter, Devon, 19, 32, 111–13, 122

Fairs, 94
Farmfield Inebriates' Reformatory, 64
Fidly, Thomas, 76
Fletcher, Anne Mary, 6
Fontmell Magna, Dorset, 11
Forton Military Prison, 125
Foundlings, 54
Four humours, 68–9
Freeman aka Foray, George, 35
French, Mark Dyer, 37
Friendly societies, 76
Friends' Ambulance Unit, 120
Frithelstock, Devon, 74
Fry, Elizabeth, 21

Galen, 68–9
Galvanism, 86
Gazette, The, 12, 34, 49

Geary, Daniel, 23
General Register of Lunatics in Asylums, 89
General Register of Protestant Dissenters, The, 12
Gepp, G.A., 88
Gerard, John, 74, 86
Germ Theory, 70, 73
Gilbert Unions, 5
Gilbert, Amy, 41
Gilbert, Ann, 41
Gilbert, Elizabeth, 41
Gilbert, Letitia, 41
Gilbert, Maria, 41
Gill, George, 79
Gill, Lydia, 79
Gill, Rebecca, 79
Gill, Richard, 79–80
Gill, Selina, 79–80
Gin Act, The, 58
Glasgow Royal Hospital for Sick Children, 75
Glasscock, Ann, 10
Glasscock, Sarah Ann, 10–11
Glasscock, Thomas, 10
Goldsmith, Mr, 32
Gornall, John, 26
Grant, Ann, 10
Grantham, John, 14
Gravesend, Kent, 12, 42
Gray, John, 100
Gray, Joshua, 99–101
Great Bedwyn, Wiltshire, 41
Great Ormond Street Hospital, 75
Green, Margaret, 25
Grimsby, Lincolnshire, 100
Grosvenor, Sarah, 64–7
Gypsy Lore Society, 98
Gypsyries, 94

Habitual Criminals' Register, 23, 27, 49
Habitual Drunkards' Lists, 23, 64

Hackney, Middlesex, 37, 89
Haine, Betty, 11
Haine, Lucy, 11
Haine, Mary, 11
Haine, Nanny, 11
Haine, William, 11
Hall, Dr Joseph, 19
Hall, Radclyffe, 111
Hann, Rev., 113
Harris's List of Covent Garden Ladies, 44
Hartland, Devon, 124–5
Haslar Hospital, 89
Hastings, Sussex, 86, 91
Heddington, Wiltshire, 2
Hellingly Asylum, 91
Herring, Alexander, 17
Hill, Charles, 17
Hill, John, 3
Hinds, Emma, 41
Hippocrates, 68
Historical Hospital Admissions Records' Project, 75
Holloway Prison, 47, 65–6
Holmes, James, 49
Holocaust, The, 35
Home office and prison commission licences, 26
Home Office Scheme, 120
Hopkins, Matthew, 106
Horton Asylum, 91–2
Hospital Records' Database, 75, 89
Howard, John, 21
Huguenot Society, 31–2
Hulks, 23–5
Hutchinson, James, 88
Hutton, Isabella, 6

Inebriates' Homes, 61
Inoculation, 71
Internet Archive, 32, 76
Isandlwana, Battle of, 124

Jamaica, 24, 36, 38–9
James I, 107
Jenner, Edward, 71
Jews, 33–5
Johnson, Robert, 49
Jones, Anthony, 111
Jones, Joan, 111
Jones, Sarah, 64–7
Justices of the Peace, 10, 15–16, 83, 86, 107

Keppel, Alice, 41
Kershaw, Eli, 22
Kettilby, Mary, 86
Keynock, Thomas Chitham, 10–11
Kingston, Jamaica, 36
Kirk Sessions, 55

Lambeth Palace Library, 17, 63
Lambeth, Surrey, 11–12, 65
Lancashire Inebriates Act Board, 61, 64
Lancaster, Lancashire, 47–8
Laud, Archbishop, 19
Laurence, Ms, 46
Lay subsidies, 32
Leake, Joan, 3
Leathern, Eli, 79–80
Leathern, William, 79–80
Leeds Industrial School, 6
Leeds, Yorkshire, 22–3, 62
Legacy of British Slave Ownership Database, 36–7, 39
Lemon, Alice, 124
Lemon, Charles John, 124
Letters of Denization, 30–2
Lewes, Sussex, 61
Lewisham, Surrey, 62
LGBTQ+, 117–19
Lincoln, Lincolnshire, 33
Lincolnshire 99–101
Lindley, Francis, 56
Lister, Joseph, 73

Liverpool, Lancashire, 6, 26–7, 35–6, 61, 66
Livesey, Joseph, 62
Lloyd, Charity, *see* Platt, Charity
Lloyd, Mary, 48
Lloyd, Robert, 48
Lloyd, Temperance, 110–13
Lock hospitals, 43
Lockhart, William, 47
London, John, 123
Lost Hospitals of London, 64, 75
Low, widow, 3
Lunacy Commission and Board of Control, 87–8
Lunacy Commission Registers, 87–8
Lunacy Law Reform Association, 86
Lying-in Hospitals, 10, 52, 75

Machin, John, 41
Madden, P.C., 41
Magdalen Hospital, Bath, 78
Magdalene Reformatories, 40
Maidstone, Kent, 25
Manchester, Jamaica, 39
Manchester, Lancashire, 46
Manorial Documents Register, 17
Market Rasen, Lincolnshire, 99–100
Martin, Susan, 79
Mayhew, Henry, 40
Maynard, Mr., 13
McDermott, Louisa, 6
McLachlan, Alexander, 49
Medical Officers of Health, 61, 76
Middle Rasen, Lincolnshire, 99
Midgley, Esther, 56
Midgley, Hannah, 56–7
Midgley, William, 56–7
Military Tribunals, 120
Millbank Prison, 27, 65
Mitcham, Surrey, 76

Mobbs, Anice, 99
Mobbs Elijah, 99
Mobbs, Emily, 99
Mobbs, Harriet, 99–101
Mobbs, Joshua, 99–101
Mobbs, Uriah, 99
Monasteries, 1, 73, 77
Montagu, Lady Mary Wortley, 71
Moore, Reginald, 123
Morris, Sarah Driscoll, 52
Museum of English Rural Life, 98

National Asylum for Idiots, 78
National Health Service, 74
National Institutions for Inebriates, 64
National Service, 120–1, 123
Naturalisations, 30–3
Nesbitt, John Coleman, 47–8
Netherton, Worcestershire, 66
Neurodiversity, 78–9, 83
Newington, Surrey, 88
Newman, George, 39
Newman, George Edward, 38–9
Newman, Richard, 39
Nicholls, George, 4
No-Conscription Fellowship, The, 120
Non-Combatant Corps, The, 120
Non-conformity, 114–17
North Willingham, Lincolnshire, 100
North, Sir Francis, 112–13

O'Neil, Susannah, 48
Ogden, John, 56
Old Bailey Online, 16, 53
Oliphant, Andrew, 17
Osberton, Nottinghamshire, 101

Paddington, Middlesex, 42
Palmer, Ann, 88
Palmer, John, 52, 74

Palmer, Mary Ann, 52
Palmer, Thomas, 88
Paré, Ambroise, 73
Parish apprentices, 55–6
Parliamentary Archives, 30
Parliamentary papers, 30
Parr, John, 41
Parr, William, 41
Passenger lists, 33
Pasteur, Louis, 70, 73
Patchett, Lizzie, 27
Paternity decrees, 55
Pearson, Karl, 29
Penance, 18–19, 55, 107
Pepys, Samuel, 72
Peterborough, Cambridgeshire, 90
Pimlico, Middlesex, 12
Plague, 70, 74
Platt, Charity, 47–9
Platt, Susan, 47
Platt, William Thomas, 47
Pleading the belly, 20
Polding, Alice, 25
Polding, Mrs W.J., 27
Policing, 22
Poole, Henry, 117
Poor houses, parish, 3
Poor Law Commission Report 1832, 5
Potter, Mr., 48
Prayer Book Rebellion, 110
Prerogativa Regis, 77
Prince Leopold, 73
Prison Registers, 23
Prisons, 20–1
Purchase, Robert, 53
Pyrotherapy, 91

Queen Victoria, 73

Ragged schools, 5–6
Railton, Ernest John, 25
Railton, Ethel, 28

Railton, Frederick, Michael, 25–8
Railton, John, 25
Rainbow, Joseph, 10
Ratcliffe, Jemima, 74
Rawson, Charles, 15
Raymond, Thomas, 112–13
Read, William, 16
Reading, Berkshire, 32
Reepham, Lincolnshire, 100
Rees, Dr George, 89
Reid, Gilbert, 55
Remenham, Berkshire, 35
Retreat, The, 90
Rigall, Mr., 100
Romany and Traveller Family History Society, 94
Romany Names, 93
Roper, Mary, 53
Rorke's Drift, 124–5
Ross, Elizabeth, 42
Rostrons, George F, 26
Rotherhithe, Surrey, 12–13
Row, Richard Henry, 45
Rowntree, Joseph, 63
Royal Society of Medicine Library, 75
Royal Victoria Hospital, 89
Rush, Benjamin, 58, 86

Salford, Lancashire, 28, 49
Scawsby, Yorkshire, 22
Scobell, Captain, 35
Scotland's Court and Criminal Database, 17
Scottish Indexes, 17
Seaman's Hospital Admissions' Records, 76
Secondat, Charles, 32
Seeds of disease, 70
Settlement:
  bonds, 11
  certificates, 11
  examinations, 9–10
  legislation, 8–11, 97
  removal orders, 10
Seven Men of Preston, The, 62
Sexuality, 117–19
Shanks, Elizabeth, 20
Sheerness, Kent, 25
Sheppey, Kent, 42
Sherbourne, Dorset, 14
Shoreditch, Middlesex, 10
Shrewsbury, Shropshire, 123
Simpson, William, 118
Skinner, James, 25
Slave registers, 35, 37, 39
Smallpox vaccination registers, 71
Smith, Frank, 10
Smith, Harriet, 99–101
Smith, John, 10, 47
Smith, Mary Ann, 10
Smith, Rosetta, 99, 100
Smith, Sarah, 22
Smith, Thomas, 10
Smith, William, 10, 22
Smith, Wisdom, 100–101
Snell, Hannah, 119
South Leith, Midlothian, 55
Southwark, Surrey, 12–13
Spakman, Mr., 3
St. Elizabeth, Jamaica, 39
St. Ives, Cornwall, 114
St. Luke's, Chelsea, Middlesex, 12
St. Martin in the Fields, Middlesex, 10
State Papers, 34, 109
Statute of Merton, 56
Stephens, Thomas, 4
Stephenson, Joseph Josiah Charles, 118–19
Stepney, Middlesex, 51
Sterne, John, 108
Stradsett, Norfolk, 35
Stratford, John, 17
Strathmiglo, Fife, 17
Suffragettes, 43, 71

Suicide, 83–4
Sunderland, Durham, 57
Surgery, black period of, 73
Sydney, Australia, 36
Sympson, William, 16
Synagogue records, 34

Taunton, Somerset, 16
Temperance movement, 62
Tempest, George, 56
Thomas , 35
Thompson, Margaret, 48
Thomson, Beak, 4
Thomson, Sebastien, 4
Thornton, James, 37
Tong, Yorkshire, 56–7
Torrington, Devon, 80
Townsend, Rev. Joseph, 4
Tranquilliser chair, 86
Transportation, 12, 24, 118
Transportation registers, 24
Trembles, Mary , 110–13
Tuke, William, 90

United Kingdom Alliance, 62–3
Usk, Monmouthshire, 42

Vaccination, 71
Vagrants, 2–3, 5, 7, 97, 99–100
Vanstone, Lily, 125
Victuallers' licences, 60
Villiers, Barbara, 40
Voluntary Hospitals' Database, 75

Wadenfield, Dr., 86
War Service, 120
Wellcome Institute, 75, 89
West Midlands Prisoner Photo Book, 64
Westminster Lying-in Hospital, 10
Whitstable, Kent, 76
Wilcox, William, 124–5
Williams, Thomas, 16
Wilson, Florence, 66
Wilson, Samuel, 66
Winder, Mr., 47
Winslade, Rachel, 110
Winson Green, Warwickshire, 65–6
Witton, Lancashire, 25
Wood Green, Middlesex, 123
Wood, George, 10
Woodford, Mr., 4
Woodhead, Hannah, 56
Woolgar, Mary Ann, 90
Woolgar, Caroline, 90
Woolgar, Philip, 90
Workhouse infirmaries, 43, 71, 76
Workhouses, 2, 5, 7, 92
Wright, Francis Charles, 15
Wylye, Wiltshire, 83

Yarnscombe, Devon, 79

Zulu Wars, 124–5